ADVANCE |
VUCA TOOLS FOR A VUCA WORLD

Dr. Deaton has the ability to use stories to help readers understand complexity and interdependence. She does this without being simplistic, which is not easy. Dr. Deaton combines head and heart in a way that nurtures our caring and challenges our thinking. It is obvious she cares about the people in the story and about you, the reader.

—Barry Johnson, creator of the Polarity Map® and principles,
author of *AND, How to Leverage Polarity, Paradox or Dilemma.*

Ann Deaton's engaging storytelling gives readers pause to reflect how they show up as leaders. Her VUCA tools offer organizations and individuals a meaningful way to continue to learn, respond, and adapt in an ever-changing landscape.

—Kirsten Siggins, co-founder Institute of Curiosity,
co-author *The Power of Curiosity*

Ann Deaton demonstrates, through an engaging and all-too-real story, the challenges of working and living in a VUCA world. She points the way to the also very real possibility of taking an empowered approach to transforming our relationship to drama—with one another and with the Volatile, Uncertain, Complex, and Ambiguous times in which we live.

—David Emerald (Womeldorff), author,
The Power of TED* (*The Empowerment Dynamic)

An engaging introduction of "VUCA" and the effects of the new normal world of volatility, uncertainty, complexity, and ambiguity on the business and personal environment. Ann's book provides some easily digestible food for thought about how to combat the alternately paralyzing and chaos-inducing effects of VUCA, and how to more effectively guide our organizations and ourselves through what promises to be a new continuous state rather than a transient passage.

—Michael McMillan, Deputy Department Head,
Space and Naval Warfare Systems Center Pacific

In this leadership fable, Ann Deaton provides a vivid depiction of the reality of leading in today's world. While her light touch is engaging, the tools and suggestions she provides are hard-hitting and get results.

—Sally Collella, co-author *Organization Network Fieldbook*

Great read for leaders and their teams struggling to find their way in a VUCA world. Ann Deaton offers a diverse set of tools, from polarity management to coaching, to help your team align and succeed.

—Holly Williams, co-author of *Being Coached: Group and Team Coaching from the Inside,* and author of *Coaching as a Culture Play: From the Inside*

Ann has created a workplace fable that is an easy read and skillfully highlights so many of the complexities experienced in today's organizations. Weaving together issues shared by many in today's fast-paced world, Ann creates a story that illustrates effectively the value of leaders reflecting inward and amongst themselves to begin to understand what is needed to deal with change. Leading the reader through the exploration of the VUCA process, the author highlights the value of constant change and the tools that will help any organization deal with change in a constructive and effective way.

—Kathy Taberner, co-founder Institute of Curiosity and
co-author *The Power of Curiosity*

What an engaging and fun story that illustrates the challenges of corporate life. The nugget you will discover in this book is how to transcend work-life drama and focus your conversations on what matters most. Every team should read this book together!

—Donna Zajonc, MCC, Dir of Coaching and Practitioner Services, Power of TED* (*The Empowerment Dynamic)

Building upon the foundation of her first book, Ann Deaton follows the same characters she developed in *Being Coached: Group and Team Coaching from the Inside.* In her new book, Ann introduces us to the concepts of VUCA (a world which is Volatile, Uncertain, Complex, and Ambiguous, aka VUCA) and how we, as leaders, must learn to respond and navigate in such a world. She focuses on the necessity of embracing a value-centered approach to leading, and the importance of leaders holding one another accountable to living (and leading) in accordance to those values. If you want to grow and evolve as a leader and as a human being, this book will serve as a thought-provoking catalyst on your journey.

—Kristin Kaufman, PCC, CLC, founder and president, Alignment, Inc.; author of the *Is This Seat Taken?* book series

This book does a great job of laying out tools to use in a VUCA world. It's clear the speed of change will not slow, and the more ways we can find to skillfully ride the wave, the better we'll do. This book is like a new surfboard!

—Lindsay Yarbrough Burr, Polarity Master and Business Consultant, The Yarbrough Group

Once again, Ann Deaton has not only captured the essence of what leaders are facing in organizations, she has also given us tools and strategies to turn these challenges into wins. Especially "people" wins. By calling out bullying and appealing to the best in all of us, she reminds us that decency goes hand in hand with success.

—Ed Stern, MSM, president, Ed Stern Leadership; founder, Start with Decency

An important question posed early in Ann's book is "Threat of VUCA or simply awareness?" There is nothing like a 1,200-pound animal to bring about awareness. Horses are gifted at mirroring back leader behaviors and intentions, and providing instant feedback. In *VUCA Tools for a VUCA World*, Jack's team has the rare opportunity to experience genuine feedback on their ineffective teamwork and to gain a profound, visceral awareness that transforms their leadership behaviors—at the farm and back at Tech Environments. Giddyup!!!

—Suzanne L. Maxwell, Equine Assisted Learning Specialist, Eponaquest Power of the Herd Instructor, leadership coach, business consultant, and PhD sociologist

When business cultures are fraught with dysfunction and miscommunication, Dr. Ann Deaton brings forward a model that focuses on possibility and healthy response. By countering the challenges within organizations with values-based leadership, collaboration, curiosity and aspiration, this framework provides traction into solution for organizations and leaders.

—Meg Rentschler, LCSW, PCC, STaR Coach Show Host

DEVELOPING LEADERS
AND TEAMS FOR
SUSTAINABLE
RESULTS

VUCA TOOLS

FOR A

VUCA W🌍RLD

ANN V. DEATON,
PhD, PCC

Printed and bound in the United States of America
ISBN: 978-0-692-07494-7
Library of Congress Control Number: 2018903783

ACKNOWLEDGMENTS

A dream you dream alone is only a dream. A dream you dream together is reality.

—John Lennon

So many people have been important in creating *VUCA Tools*™. Thanks go to Judy and Nicholas, as always, for your unconditional love and your supportive and challenging feedback. Love and appreciation also go to my nuclear and extended family—my siblings, Dad, stepmom, uncles and aunts, and cousins. Deep gratitude to my "Coaching Cronies," four friends who have been a part of my circle of trust for many years now. And I am indebted to my other communities of learning—Barry and Cliff, and my Polarities Mastery cohort VI, Donna and David and all our TED* practitioner colleagues, Judith and our C-IQ community. Thank you to all the clients I have had the honor to work with—individual leaders, teams, organizations, and communities—and to all my own coaches along the way. I so appreciate learning with and from each of you. Thanks to Bethany Kelly and Publishing Partner, as well as to editor Frank Steele. Your input contributed to this book being better than it would have otherwise been. There are many others who've been a part of this, and I trust that I have thanked each of you individually more than once. I always recognize that I am "building on the shoulders of giants" in all the work I do, and I trust I have done justice to your contributions.

CONTENTS

PREFACE

VUCA is a term introduced by the U.S. Army War College in the 1990s to describe the dramatically altered circumstances in which military leaders had to operate. VUCA is an acronym for Volatile, Uncertain, Complex, Ambiguous. The proven ways that leaders had learned to operate on the battlefield were no longer adequate to the evolving challenges they faced.[1]

The acronym VUCA has since been applied in the business world to understand the similarly challenging environment in which companies now operate. We are in a fast-changing world that pushes all of us past our limits. Our business leaders and teams are short on time, energy, and resources, yet there is no sign that the rate of change is slowing down. If anything, it is on the increase. Enter *VUCA Tools for a VUCA World*.

The more I thought about VUCA, the more I thought that leaders need more than just the awareness of Volatility, Uncertainty, Complexity, and Ambiguity to be effective. They must have tools and strategies that enable them not just to survive but to thrive in the face of the changing terrain. *VUCA Tools for a VUCA World* is the result of my recognizing how leaders and teams benefit from specific tools that enable their success. *VUCA Tools* begins with the fictional tale of one group of leaders as they experience VUCA together and struggle to discover stable ground to move forward effectively again. The characters in the book each have their own individual issues (as do we all), and their company, Tech Environments, is in a highly competitive, rapidly changing industry. It is a recipe for failure unless the leaders are open to learning about themselves, developing fresh visions for success, and embracing new perspectives and approaches for sustainable results. This is the story of how Tech Environments strives to implement and co-create strategies for succeeding in the long term. Please join the team as they take on the challenge of VUCA and see where the journey takes them, and you.

And by the way, if you recognize any of the leaders in this book, it may be that you read my previous book: *Being Coached: Group and Team Coaching from the Inside*[2] (co-authored by Holly Williams). Other than that, any resemblances between *VUCA Tools'* characters and the characters you've met along the way are completely coincidental.

Ann V. Deaton, PhD, PCC, February 2018

INTRODUCTION

When reading a book, I sometimes skip the Introduction and Preface, and I suspect I'm not the only one. However, I often return to the first part later to get additional context. Whatever your approach, here are a few details and suggestions that will enable you to use *VUCA Tools* more effectively.

First, the layout of the book. Parts 1 and 2 tell the story of Tech Environments and its team. Some call this a business fable (but I read an HBR article[3] a few years back which said that the business fable is done, so that could be risky). I just call it a story, a tale of what can happen in any company when the external climate changes and the habits the organization and its people have fallen into no longer work the way they once did.

- Part 1 highlights Tech Environments' leaders and team and their sense of dismay and overwhelm at the challenges they are experiencing. Each leader has different reactive tendencies as they face a new set of demands: demands for different products, greater civility and accountability in the workplace, evolving models for how to lead, customers' high expectations, and a dramatically increased quantity of information to process. In sum: VUCA.

- Part 2 follows the team as they explore and adopt various tactics for thriving in this VUCA world. The approaches shared all offer antidotes to VUCA, each tapping into one or more of the VUCA Tools™: Values, Us, Curiosity, and Aspirations. Whether they are learning how to think in Both/And terms, being transparent and vulnerable when they make mistakes, or considering the neuroscience behind why people do what they do, the leaders all have their own favorite approaches. As a team, they also must create alignment and common ground so they can move forward together.

- Part 3 includes notes to elaborate on details from the story without detracting from the flow of the story itself. Part 3 also delivers a few focused topical chapters for those of you who want to take a deeper dive. You can use Part 3 to examine the four VUCA tools in more detail as they are embodied throughout the book, or explore the tools' application to your own VUCA context through individual and team exercises, additional reading, podcasts, and reflection. Whether you are a coach, a leader, an HR or OD practitioner, or all of the above, you'll see options for application.

Second, a little more about the characters. The team at Tech Environments was introduced several years ago in *Being Coached: Group and Team Coaching from the Inside*. Like all of us, they have grown and changed since we last saw them. Here's a brief description of who's who at Tech Environments, in order of their appearance in the book:

- **Donna**, Chief Marketing Officer, arrived at the company and joined its senior leadership team four years earlier. In her role, Donna cares a great deal about what people think.
- **Arun**, Chief Technology Officer and Chief Operating Officer, has been at Tech Environments for over a decade and has, shall we say, a reputation.
- **Lynn**, Chief Risk Officer, took over for Edgar three years earlier when he left the company due to a family issue. Lynn takes her job very seriously.
- **Ted**, Chief Financial Officer, has been at Tech Environments for longer than he can remember. He thinks about retiring, but keeps finding new reasons to stay.

- **Jen**, the newest hire on the finance team. She is talented and is beginning to find her voice.
- **Javy**, also on the finance team, loves to scan the external economic environment for trends that could affect Tech Environments.
- **Pete**, finance team lead, prides himself on being a penny-pincher on behalf of Tech Environments. Pete has a couple of young kids at home that he is still figuring out.
- **Patrick**, Chief People Officer, assumed his role almost three years ago when his boss Ellen left Tech Environments for a bigger gig. Patrick wishes she were still there.
- **Jack**, CEO of Tech Environments, is a worrier and a powerhouse, determined not to let Tech Environments fail. Jack is close to having an empty nest at home, and still learning.
- **Kim** is a program manager on Arun's team. She was part of an earlier group and peer coaching initiative at Tech Environments (described in *Being Coached*) that helped her make a successful transition back to work after staying home with her kids for several years.
- **Edgar**, a sustainability consultant, had been promoted to Chief Risk Officer at Tech Environments four years ago, but decided to leave the company soon afterwards. Edgar is back for a visit, or maybe more.
- **Jordan**, a leadership and team coach, has worked with Tech Environments off and on for years. She is a trusted partner to many of its leaders.
- **Raj** is a technical guy. Like Kim, he participated in a high-potentials coaching group at Tech Environments several years earlier. In the process, Raj fell in love with neuroscience and has become the resident expert others come to.
- **Charles**, a previously overwhelmed project lead, who used coaching in the past to create a better work-life balance for himself so he could love his work again.

- **Marianne** is Senior Training Manager at Tech Environments. On the HR team, she reports to Patrick. Like several of the other midlevel managers, Marianne participated in the peer and group coaching initiative a few years earlier. She got good at asserting herself, and now does so with ease and humor.

Third, do it your way. As you read *VUCA Tools*, feel free to read the story in Parts 1 and 2, and just skim the didactic chapters at the end. Or you can highlight possible solutions to your own VUCA dilemmas throughout the book. A few of you may even create tables and mind maps of the content, or pull out chapters to share as case studies with your own teams. My hope is that you'll enjoy drawing on your own experiences, preferences, and knowledge throughout the book, making it uniquely yours. Different readers are drawn to different tools. Our best responses to our VUCA world emerge when we engage in reciprocity, sharing with one another our own unique perspectives and listening to and learning from others. I'd love to hear what you discover and create. Growth comes from expanding the way we see. Enjoy.

VUCA Tools for a VUCA World: Developing Leaders and Teams for Sustainable Results

Ann V. Deaton

PART 1

WHAT'S UP WITH TECH ENVIRONMENTS?

1

THE WRITING ON THE WALL

Donna sat down at her usual table and sipped her favorite latte. She loved this time of the morning and the chance to launch her day in a lively coffee shop before heading to her demanding job as Chief Marketing Officer at Tech Environments. Seeing the opportunity to catch up on her reading, Donna pulled out her briefcase and an industry magazine she liked for its brief articles and vivid writing style.

A few minutes later, Donna was shaking her head in dismay. She couldn't believe what she was reading. The short article in *Tech Consulting Review* was devastating. Its title—"The Slow and Painful Death of Technology Consulting"—was frightening enough. Even more terrifying was the fact that her own company, Tech Environments, was cited as an example of a "formerly prosperous company now on the downslide." Her heart racing, Donna wished she could find and hide all the issues of the trade magazine. *That pretty much trashes everything I've done to build credibility and business this quarter. I guess even if I could destroy all the copies, it still wouldn't get rid of the online version, or the social media buzz. We're toast. And won't Lynn be delighted to point out that I should have had the pulse of the market before this came out?*

Leaving her latte behind, Donna headed for her car. She drove slowly toward Tech Environments, wondering what kind of damage control she needed to do. Her phone buzzed several times, but she ignored the calls. Donna suspected that the rest of the leadership team, or at least Lynn, Tech Environments' Chief Risk Officer, were hearing about the article themselves. "No point responding until I get there," she mumbled. "It's not as if I know what to do."

2

ARUN IS IN HIS OWN LITTLE WORLD

A run was running late again, and kicking himself for choosing this morning to do a longer workout. Given his dual role as CTO and COO at Tech Environments, Arun knew he had no time to train for a half marathon. However, both his wife and his direct reports had informed him he was a bear when he didn't make time to work out. Without a goal like the half marathon, Arun had never been able to commit to a regular workout schedule. Being late was the cost.

Now he stood impatiently outside the gym waiting for his Lyft ride to arrive. Finally (nearly three minutes later, he noted), the car pulled up and Arun got in. Ignoring the driver, he pulled out his phone.

"Calendar, what's my schedule look like this morning?" he inquired of his phone.

"According to your calendar," the robotic voice intoned, "you have a meeting with Lynn at 9, a vendor demo at 10, and a peer coaching meeting over lunch with Patrick. Shall I go on?"

"No, never mind." Arun was typically abrupt, and was glad that his calendar app didn't seem to take offense.

Scrolling through the contacts on his phone, Arun chose Patrick's number and pressed the Call button. When Patrick didn't pick up, Arun dictated a message: "Don't really have anything for our peer coaching today, Patrick. Let's cancel and focus on what's really important."

Over the past several years, Arun had come to accept the commitment to a coaching culture at Tech Environments. He even acknowledged that on occasion his peer coaching with Chief People Officer Patrick was somewhat useful. When in a time crunch, however, Arun always found it easy to prioritize other aspects of his dual role as Chief Operating Officer and Chief Technology Officer. Today, he was hoping that Patrick would accept his proposal to cancel.

Just as he was thinking this, Arun's message chime sounded. "No dice, Arun. Can't cancel today. I've got something important and need your brilliant coaching. See you at 12."

"It was worth a try," Arun mumbled to himself. "I wonder what Patrick has going on. I really thought he was beginning to feel settled in to his role since Ellen left a couple of years back. I was convinced he didn't have enough experience, but he's been better than I expected. Anyway, he's a good recruiter. He sure keeps my teams well-staffed."

"Huh?" asked the driver.

"I'm not talking to you," Arun responded. Catching the driver's glare in the rearview mirror, Arun apologized, "Ah, sorry, didn't mean to be rude. I was just talking to myself."

The Lyft driver shrugged and focused on the traffic. "Suit yourself. It wouldn't cost you to be civil." He slowed down and pulled up to the main entrance of Tech Environments.

Striding toward the building, Arun confirmed the Lyft charge on his phone, choosing the box indicating $0 for the tip. "Here's a tip for you," he glanced toward the departing car. "Don't give social skills lectures to important people." Whistling, Arun swiped his magnetic card at the entrance and marched into the reception area, narrowly avoiding a collision with Lynn.

3

WHEN RISK IS REALITY

Ducking out of Arun's path, Lynn touched his shoulder as he kept moving through the lobby. "Whoa there, Arun! Where's the fire?"

Coming from Tech Environments' Chief Risk Officer, this made Arun laugh. "Leave it to you to see a risk in a guy rushing to get to his desk in the morning, Lynn. No fire, just a few things on my plate."

"We've got a problem. Got a minute?" Lynn inquired.

"I really don't, Lynn. Can't it wait until our senior leadership team strategy session tomorrow?" Arun was clearly reluctant to prolong their conversation.

Lynn shook her head. "No, it really can't. I think you are going to want to hear this now and spend the day figuring out how it affects your strategy for the business. It's not good."

A pair of analysts nearby turned, clearly curious about what Lynn was saying.

Suddenly aware that they were talking in a public place, Lynn motioned Arun toward the elevator. "Come on. Let's head to my office to talk. We can stop for coffee, and tea for you, on our way."

Seated in her office a few minutes later with their mugs, Lynn pulled up the article from the *Tech Consulting Review* and projected it onto the wall monitor. Tapping on the desk, she remarked, "I think you have our

Chief Marketing Officer to thank for this. Donna let us get blindsided." The article on "The Slow and Painful Death of Technology Consulting" came into focus, and Lynn highlighted two lines: "Tech Environments no longer stands out as an innovator. Clients can implement existing systems on their own."

"Oh, crap," Arun muttered, as he scanned the short article. "This is a disaster."

"I can talk to our lawyer, Arun. We might be able to get a retraction," Lynn proposed.

Arun brandished his spoon as he finished stirring sugar into his tea. "What could you tell the lawyer, Lynn, that would give him any ammunition? It's hard to prove we are innovative." After a pause, he continued, "To be honest, we have been losing ground. We just can't seem to keep up. I'd like to blame Ted's financial conservatism, but the truth is that our clients have more problems than we can solve. Much of the time we encourage them to keep their legacy systems—at least they already know how to use them. We used to add so much value to our clients' businesses. They still trust us as partners, but they aren't willing to spend a significant part of their budgets on our consulting services unless we bring something unexpected and new. I can't say I blame them."

Lynn didn't immediately respond. She wasn't used to seeing Arun this subdued, and wasn't sure what to say. "What are you going to do about it, Arun? It's not like you to sit back and give up. You are one of the most determined leaders I know. In any case, everyone is going to blame Donna, as well they should."

Arun just shook his head as he stood. "Rough morning," he observed in a dejected tone. "Oh well. I've got a peer coaching session with Patrick at noon. He'll be happy I'm bringing something juicy for us to coach on. Thanks for the tea, and for giving me the heads-up on the article. I'd rather not be uninformed." Nodding to Lynn, Arun got up and disappeared out the door.

4

MONEY DOESN'T GROW ON TREES

The finance team filed in around the conference table, and Ted began, "You've all posted your reports on expenses and revenues, as well as how we're doing year over year. What do we need to cover today?"

As a result of their team coaching work with Jordan a few years previously, Ted had become accustomed to depending on his team members to do their jobs. He trusted them to know what was important to share when the team gathered for their biweekly finance review meetings, and typically started with a question. Everyone in the room knew this was a time that their CFO encouraged them to consider the big picture, take risks, and pose questions.

The newest team member, Jen, half-raised her hand, and Ted nodded for her to take the floor.

"I've only been here a couple of years," Jen began. "Over that period, I've noticed that we seldom fail to meet our revenue targets, certainly not for more than one quarter. This makes three consecutive quarters of not making our targets. I suspect we are all aware of that? I guess I'm wondering if there's anything we can do about it, other than report it accurately, I mean." Jen ended a little uncertainly, and quickly sat down.

"Thank you, Jen. Anyone else?" Ted asked.

"I'll go," Javy volunteered. "I scan the *Wall Street Journal* every day, and it seems like there's a lot of negativity on technology consulting. I know maybe our consulting services at Tech Environments focus a little more broadly than just technology solutions, but I've just been curious about the industry. It seems like a lot of client companies see us as a cost and don't see the potential for profit. Everyone talks about cost savings with technology, but no one talks about trying to increase our clients' revenues. Are we missing the boat?"

"Good question, Javy. As with Jen, I'm impressed to hear what you are thinking about. Who else?"

Pete quickly volunteered. "Well, this may not be popular, but I guess I'll say it anyway. I see how much Jack and our senior leadership team seem to like coaching, and Patrick certainly highlights it as a significant benefit when we recruit employees. The thing is, we've already done coaching. It's had some good effects, I agree, but why are we still paying Jordan a retainer? Shouldn't we be fixed by now? The line item for coaching is just as big as our training budget. That seems like way too much to be spending on coaching. At least with training, our team earns the certifications that prove our credibility to our clients. We could save a chunk of money if we deleted the coaching line item." Pete sat down, looking pleased with himself.

PERFORMANCE: THREE CONSECUTIVE QUARTERS OF NOT MEETING REVENUE

RELEVANCE: OVER-FOCUS ON COST REDUCTION, LITTLE ON INCREASING REVENUES

STEWARDSHIP: ARE WE SPENDING ON THE RIGHT THINGS—E.G., SHOULD WE BE SPENDING LESS ON COACHING, MORE ON CERTIFICATIONS?

"All great observations, team. I've captured them on our whiteboard here."

Ted again addressed the group, "Have I captured these correctly?" He looked at those who had expressed their concerns—Jen and Pete agreed with Ted's synthesis. Javy added, "For the second one, I meant specifically for our clients—what are we doing to help *them* increase their revenues? They see us as a cost, so what are we doing to offset that expense? I don't think it should be cost savings alone. We are pretty pricey."

Ted acknowledged Javy's clarification. Then he challenged the group again, "So what do you want to do? We aren't consultants ourselves; we're the finance team. We aren't delivering directly to Tech Environments' clients. What actions can we take in our support function to help the company? I know you all see things that others don't. Give it some thought, and come next time with your recommendations for action steps."

Ted smiled at the animated sound of his team's conversations as they left the conference room. *I really do love mentoring them,* he thought. *It's the reason I've stayed at Tech Environments this long. I hope it will make a difference to us now.*

5

IT'S NOT ABOUT YOU

Patrick and Arun usually scheduled their peer coaching conversations over lunch, a habit that, on busy days, often ensured that they actually got to eat lunch. If possible, they ate outside. Today's weather was pleasant, but it looked as if it might rain, so the pair chose a small team table under an overhang.

As they were sitting down, Arun opened, "You said you had something today, and now something's come up for me too. I'll go first."

Patrick raised an eyebrow before responding, "Usually, Arun, I'd be fine with that, but as it happens, there's something I need your coaching on today, and I'd like to start with me. Okay with you?"

Arun acquiesced, though his grimace indicated he wasn't happy about it.

Ignoring Arun's obvious irritation, Patrick began. "I want to remind you, Arun, that we have an agreement that anything we talk about is confidential. Even if I tell you something that you want to tell Jack or others, the only way I can trust you is if it stays between us until I decide to share it myself. Agreed?"

Wow. It must be bad if our Chief People Officer is worried about confidentiality, Arun thought. Aloud, he replied, "Yes, that's our agreement, and I understand its importance. What is it you want to talk about?"

Patrick took a deep breath before he spoke. "As you know, I've been very committed to leadership development and coaching since I first arrived almost a decade ago. Ellen was a great manager for me, and I learned a lot from her. I was sorry to see her go. The last couple of years have been a good opportunity for me to take control and experiment as I've stepped into playing a bigger role here. The truth is, however, that I'm pretty lonely. People keep secrets from me because of my role. And in this year when our revenues are down, I worry that you and Jack and Ted all see my department as a drain. That attitude makes my job doubly hard." Patrick stopped abruptly and glanced at Arun before continuing. "I have an offer from another company. They heard me do a presentation on our internal coaching for managers program at the Association for Talent Development conference recently, and they were impressed. Their budget for human capital development is one I couldn't begin to dream of here. The salary is good, and they're not expecting me to be a senior leader. I think I'd have friends at work again. They are committed to my growth, and even offering to fund my education to earn my leadership coaching certification. That's about a $20K bonus. Even better than all those perks, I'd be working with and learning from Ellen again. The job is with the company she went to when she left here. It's an offer I'm seriously considering."

Arun, normally quick with a comment or question, sat quietly for a moment before responding. "If this weren't our peer coaching time, I'd be giving you my opinion and advice. I'd tell you to stay put and forget the mentoring and training. You already know enough. However, it's clear you are feeling unsure, and in any case, you didn't ask what I thought; you said you wanted some peer coaching. I know that means I have to deliberately set aside whatever I think and let this be about you. At least I've learned that much over the past few years," he declared. "So, I guess I'll ask you a question—what have you thought about so far?"

Patrick sighed. "I've thought about loyalty, and how everyone would see me as a traitor, leaving when the chips are down. I've thought about fear, and wondered whether I'd be chickening out. I've also thought about just crafting my resignation letter to Jack and submitting it."

"What else?" Arun prompted.

"Well, I've also been thinking about myself as a leader, and what a leader would do. For such a long time, I've seen myself as 'in development,' a high potential who still has a lot to learn. Sometimes I have a feeling all of us have a lot to learn, and that you never know everything. I just try things, hope they work, and learn from the ones that don't. So I guess I've been considering that too, that maybe I'll never be 100 percent infallible." Patrick pulled out his planner and glanced at some of his notes.

"Anything else?" Arun asked.

"I guess it could be important to actually think about what success is for me. I mean, I used to think it was being part of the senior leadership team. But I've accomplished that, and I'm still not happy. Maybe it's being well thought of, being seen as a resource instead of as a cost center. And even as I say that, I wonder if it's just about *feeling* like a leader. I mean, it's not as if any of you have challenged my expense budget more than anyone else's. Maybe I just need to get more internally confident and stop looking for others' approval."

"Sounds like you might have something there," Arun acknowledged. "At least you seem more energetic when you say that. So, what's your next step?"

"I'm not sure, Arun, but I don't think it's giving Jack my resignation letter. At least not yet. You've helped me to think about some things. I didn't really think you'd be a very good peer coach for me when we started because you're so definite about everything, as if there's just one right way. But you have really developed a knack for asking questions, and it helps. Thanks." Glancing at his watch, Patrick looked startled. "Wow. I apologize, Arun, but I really have to go. And we didn't take any time for your concern."

"I'm sure I've done that to you at least a few times," Arun chuckled. "So I probably deserve it. But actually, you reminded me that sometimes we think things are urgent, and maybe they are, but not necessarily the most important thing to focus on. I'm glad we kept our attention on you today. It gave me a chance to see again that listening can be an action. I'm not really built for just listening, so it's a good reminder. See you tomorrow at our strategy session. Good luck with figuring out your next steps."

"Thanks, Arun. I'll see you bright and early at the off-site tomorrow." Both men stood and tossed the remnants of their lunches into the trash before setting off in opposite directions.

6

THE THREAT FACING
TECH ENVIRONMENTS

The next morning, Jack scanned the room, taking in each member of the Tech Environments senior leadership team. Ted, Lynn, Arun, Donna, and Patrick all stared back at him, waiting expectantly. They had cleared their packed schedules for this day of visioning and strategic planning. Everyone was expecting the investment to pay off. After the past few days of bad news, the timing of this meeting seemed especially crucial.

Jack cleared his throat and began in an unusually formal way. "As CEO of Tech Environments, I'm disturbed about the state of our company and worried about our future. This week, we got some bad media attention, as you all are aware."

Lynn frowned, glancing in Donna's direction.

Jack continued. "However, the press is just one of many indicators that we have a problem. Our client engagement numbers are down, as are our revenues. We have no fresh products and few new customers in the pipeline. Human capital is an issue too. We've recently lost two high-potential leaders who were part of our succession plan, and I can't even begin to guess at how many quality employees have moved on. I'm sure Patrick could tell us exact numbers, but that's not the point. The way we've been operating up until now doesn't seem to be working anymore, at least not very well. The scope of engagements, the expectations our customers have of us to be experts at everything, the rapid changes in technology are unbelievable. Our team is frazzled, which isn't a setup for creative thinking. I have to admit that I don't have a clue about where we should be focusing as we create our 3- to 5-year plan." Jack gazed down at his notes as Ted and Donna exchanged looks of concern.

"I've listed on the board here what I think are the problems we need to be solving in our session today, or at least figuring out an approach to tackle." Jack gestured at the board:

THE PROBLEMS WE'RE FACING:

1. A ROLLER COASTER OF UNPREDICTABLE CHANGE

2. LIMITED PROOF OF THE VALUE WE BRING AND RESULTANT LOSS OF CONFIDENCE

3. COMPLICATED, MULTIFACETED PROJECTS, DEMANDS, AND CLIENTS

4. NO LONGER CLEAR ABOUT WHERE WE ARE HEADED

Everyone looked up at the board, as Patrick and Donna jotted down the list.

Patrick commented first, "You haven't included the people problems, Jack. I heard you mention retention and morale as issues."

"Definitely a concern," responded Jack, "but I have the sense it may be the result of these issues I've listed and not the primary problem. Obviously, I'm open to other perspectives."

Lynn spoke up now. "Well, we aren't the first company to deal with VUCA," she commented. "What are other companies doing?"

All eyes shifted to Lynn now, with expressions ranging from confusion to curiosity.

"Huh?" Arun queried.

"VUCA," Lynn repeated. "You know—Volatile, Uncertain, Complex, Ambiguous. The new reality of constant change. We're not dealing with anything different from any other business these days. VUCA is the new normal."

Ted scratched his head. "I've heard something about that. I think there was an article in *HBR*[4] or something. What does VUCA have to do with us and this meeting today?"

Jack held up his hand. "Wait a minute here. You mean there is a name for all this chaos? Am I the only one who's clueless about this?" Patrick, Arun, and Donna all shook their heads. Jack continued with energy, "Well I, for one, would like to hear more about this VUCA thing."

Several of the team chuckled at Jack's sudden intensity. Their laughter was a welcome release from the tension they'd felt since the moment they'd arrived at the off-site. Ted glanced at Lynn and gestured to her to take the lead. "You're the Chief Risk Officer, Lynn. I think you are in the best position to describe the threat VUCA poses to Tech Environments, not to mention its impact on the whole technology industry."

But before Lynn could get started, Arun interrupted. "I'm sure this whatever acronym you said is interesting and all, but didn't we set aside this day so we could make some progress on our strategy? I don't want to get into a theoretical discussion and walk out of here with nothing to show for our time. As COO and CTO, I have better things to do." Realizing how he sounded, Arun added, "I'm sure we all do."

Patrick was always vigilant to the team's interactions. The ever-diplomatic Chief People Officer, he immediately put himself in Jack's camp, "Let's take a quick vote. Would it be helpful to others besides Jack and me to hear a little more about what Lynn was saying? It sounds like those are some of the issues Jack was starting with anyway, even if he didn't have a name for it. Maybe knowing what this 'VUCA' is gives us a place to begin today. Who's up for a little tutorial from Lynn, and anything from Ted that he remembers from what he's read about it?"

All nodded, though Arun still looked unconvinced.

Ted quickly reached for his computer and located the HBR article he had mentioned. "I've just sent you all a link to the article," he said. "All of us reading it is likely to be more useful than me trying to recollect what I read."

"I'll jot down the basics of VUCA to get us started," Lynn said, and got up quickly to go to the whiteboard .

VUCA
V-VOLATILE
U-UNCERTAIN
C-COMPLEX
A-AMBIGUOUS

ARMY WAR COLLEGE TERM, CIRCA 1990, NOW PROMINENTLY USED TO CAPTURE THE CHALLENGES FACED BY BUSINESS LEADERS
THREAT OF VUCA, OR SIMPLY AWARENESS?

Jack continued to gaze at the board for several moments before commenting, "That's great, Lynn. Very helpful just to see it spelled out. And I applaud your final question about awareness versus threat. We know from Jordan, and from our colleague Raj, that we can get triggered when we feel threatened. We tend to go into survival mode, and react by trying to escape, deny, or defend ourselves against the threat. Lately I think we've been frozen in place, hunkered down and in denial, just hoping it gets better. It's not what I want for us as leaders. I know we can thrive again at Tech Environments. I also realize that we have a lot of questions right now and a challenging environment we must learn to respond to differently. We don't have much time. Let's take the next hour to read the article Ted just sent us, and to consider some of our current challenges in the light of VUCA. I'd like us to produce a plan for next steps, and at least one or two strategies we can all use to keep ourselves grounded and connected as we move forward. Focus on how we can take action with VUCA, instead of focusing on the threat itself," he reminded them.

The group spread out around the conference table and began to read on their laptops, jot notes, or study what Lynn and Jack had written on the whiteboards. When lunch arrived an hour later, most glanced up in surprise at how quickly the time had passed.

7

DONNA TAKES THE LEAD

After lunch, the entire senior leadership team reconvened around the table.

"What does everyone think?" Jack asked. "Where do we go from here?"

"How about we take a week to identify our strategic priorities? Nail down the big picture before we get mired in the details?" Ted offered.

Lynn weighed in, "I'm with Ted. I suggest we take a week and go back to our departments and see what our teams can come up with. There is a lot of risk to be managed, and getting our teams to weigh in makes the most sense. Meanwhile, I think we need to hear Donna's explanation for how she allowed us to be put in such a negative light in the press. We all need to understand how Marketing is managing our reputation." Lynn could not help feeling the Chief Marketing Officer had put them all in a difficult position.

"Maybe we should bring Jordan in again to coach our team. She's been very effective in the past," Patrick proposed. "And we are starting to struggle with our teamwork again."

"I believe we are experiencing the normal variation we've undergone in the past," Arun stated. "Yes, we received a bit of negative press recently, but we know we have a sound set of approaches and loyal clients who are not going anywhere. I suggest we ride out the storm the way we always have. One of my project teams is confident they will be selling an additional project to one of our bigger clients imminently. They've come up with a new approach to solve an issue for the client. It's turning around, and we should stay the course."

Jack glanced at Arun in surprise. "That might be the first time I've ever heard you suggest that we keep doing what we've been doing, Arun. It's not like you."

Jack still wanted to get everyone's input. "Donna?" he prompted.

Donna spoke up now. Still feeling stung by Lynn's earlier comment, Donna announced, "Based on our conversation so far, it's obvious a lot of pieces go into what makes up our reputation. Some of that is my job, of course, and other aspects belong to all of us. I have a suggestion for us moving forward. We've been involved in this single-minded pursuit of understanding the numerous problems facing us, all the issues we are worried about. That's valuable, of course, but I suggest we shift our emphasis. Let's take advantage of the few hours we have left today." Having captured the room's attention, she continued confidently, "As Jack has pointed out, becoming too preoccupied with all the threats we're facing impedes our ability to think clearly. We'd benefit more by devoting our energy and attention to where we want to be headed. What's our vision? What do we see in the future? A lack of vision is listed as one of our problems; I'd recommend that we see it as an opportunity as well. That's what we do with our clients, and the same approach would be valuable for us."

Engaged by Donna's sudden intensity, several members of the team applauded. Jack sat down and encouraged Donna, "It sounds like you have something in mind. Why don't you take us through this part?"

With Donna's guidance, the team worked hard for the next few hours, identifying the measurable outcomes they envisioned for Tech Environments. Lynn seemed to put her irritation with Donna aside and contributed as freely as the rest of the team. By the end of the session, Donna had highlighted the six desired results the team had agreed on:

1. A set of clear and relevant values that give us a road map to work and live by
2. An engaged team of associates who see themselves as problem solvers and want to be here
3. An updated and expanded set of products and methodologies to offer our clients
4. Leaders who are role models for the values we espouse
5. Robust revenues that enable confidence and growth
6. Positive visibility in the press regarding our culture and our positive impact for our clients and community

Patrick's face fell as he looked at the list. "This is a lot to do. It's every aspect of our business, both internal and external. How are we going to accomplish that, as busy as we are?"

In contrast, Jack sounded more hopeful now, "As I look at this list, it seems like a strong response to VUCA. We'd be on solid ground to respond to its challenges." He closed the session with a request to each of the other senior leaders. "This has been a demanding day, and I know you all are tired. In the spirit of focusing on our key outcomes, I'd like you each to identify what we already have in place that aligns with these desired results. For instance, Arun, you indicated earlier that one of your project managers has a new approach that a client is interested in. That would support several of the metrics we've outlined for success. Let's come back with data about existing initiatives and examples."

Everyone nodded, and began to get up and gather their materials. Only Lynn and Arun hesitated, unconvinced that they had a viable path forward.

8

DOES PATRICK NEED A FRIEND?

I guess I'm looking for someone to tell me what to do, Patrick thought as he walked to his car in the parking garage. *I feel like by now I should be more confident, that I should be inspiring others' confidence. But there's so much I don't know, and everything is changing so quickly. It's not just technology; it's the people side of things too. I wonder if I'm the only one who realizes that. That new job offer, and working with my old boss Ellen again, looks better and better.*

As Patrick clicked his remote to unlock his car, he glanced at the rear of the car. "Oh no!" he spoke aloud this time. "Just my luck. Maybe it's a warning my time here is up!"

"Talking to yourself again?" The voice behind him startled Patrick. Kim was grinning, "My kids say I do that too, but I had no idea our Chief People Officer was just as whacko. I hear talking to yourself is not a good sign. . . ." Kim's voice trailed off as she saw the troubled expression on Patrick's face. "Whoa, Patrick, I'm just kidding. Really."

Patrick took a deep breath. *I need to get myself together*, he thought, then muttered. "Ah, Kim, it's nothing. Just realized my tire is flat. Guess I need to call a tow truck."

"Yep, it's flat all right," Kim said, "but it seems like something else is going on. Do you want to talk while you're waiting for that tow truck?"

Wondering whether that was a good idea, Patrick found himself agreeing to Kim's suggestion. "Sure, that would be great. I feel like I got to know you last year when you were on the culture task group I led. I'd like to catch up. Let me call this in first."

Patrick turned to Kim as he got off the phone. "You may want to change your mind. They say it's going to be an hour before they can get out here."

"I really don't mind, Patrick. My ex has the kids tonight and I was just headed home to an uncharacteristically quiet house. I've got time." Kim smiled and gestured to the covered shuttle shelter. "Want to sit while we wait?"

The two found a bench just outside the garage where they could sit and watch for the tow truck. "What's going on, Patrick?" Kim asked. "Last year you always seemed upbeat and excited about how we were growing our workplace culture. Today you look anything but upbeat—almost downtrodden."

Patrick nodded in agreement and then began hesitantly, "You've been part of our culture work, Kim. There is something I'd like to ask you about. I've been concerned that we are no longer viewed as a positive place to work. Have you perceived any cultural issues in your recent experience? Harassment, bullying . . . stuff like that?" Without waiting for her answer, Patrick continued, "Do you know Glassdoor—the online job search site?" At Kim's noncommittal shrug, he continued, "It's a site that a lot of job seekers check when they are applying to a company. One of the things Glassdoor does is collect reviews from current and previous employees. When Tech Environments gets reviewed well, it makes our recruiting easier. On the flip side, of course, negative critiques hurt us. Three recent reviews have got me worried. They cite cons in working here that include problems with bullying in our culture. Unfortunately, two are from current employees, so I suspect we might have a real issue. It's not just sour grapes from someone who went to work elsewhere." Patrick looked up at the end of this long monologue to see Kim's reaction.

She looked concerned, and decided to probe. "Did they actually use the term 'bully'? That seems like such a schoolyard kind of word."

"Not all of them," Patrick admitted. "One said that he, or she, had felt intimidated. Another used the phrase 'unfairly targeted,' and a third said they were 'bullied repeatedly.' There aren't that many reviews about us on Glassdoor, so it seems like a pretty strong theme. And definitely not what we want to be known for! I blame myself if bullying is going on and I haven't known about it or done anything to address it." The troubled look on Patrick's face had returned. "What do you think, Kim?"

Now it was Kim's turn to look uneasy. When she didn't immediately respond, Patrick pressed, "Kim, I could use your honest assessment."

"Okay, Patrick. I don't think it's what you want to hear, but it could be what you need to hear. I have a couple of data points. One of the men on the senior leadership team is seen as a bit of a bully by a few people I've spoken with." Kim hesitated. "Well, I might as well be clear—the leader people see as a bully is Arun. For the most part, associates don't see him as badly intentioned or deliberately threatening, but they do feel browbeaten by Arun's abrupt and direct style. If he occasionally praised them or gave them visible credit, the perception might be offset, but you know Arun—he just goes on to the next challenge and badgers people to step up again. At the end of the day, folks end up feeling bruised. They are getting burned out, and looking for opportunities elsewhere." Kim stopped talking, expecting a reaction from Patrick.

"Okay," he paused. "I'm unhappy to hear that, and nonetheless it is helpful to have more substance to the Glassdoor comments. So, Kim, you mentioned a couple of data points. Is there something else?"

"I'm afraid so, Patrick. Women here are frequently harassed when they attempt to prioritize their families. I noticed it when I first came back to work a few years ago—several women gave me advice along the lines of 'Make sure you don't mention your kids to the boss,' and 'Don't ever say you are leaving early to get your son to soccer practice.' I took their counsel for the most part, but even so I can remember being ridiculed a couple of times when I chose to go to a school assembly or field day instead of staying late at work. When I say ridiculed, I would tell you it occasionally verged on being threatened or intimidated. One project lead told me he was listing me in his weekly update report as a 'poor performer.' And someone told me later he had badmouthed me in a team meeting, and no one had the courage to disagree with him. I've managed to deal with the fallout of being a mother, but there shouldn't be any fallout. It does feel like harassment at times. Women employees here are certainly sensitive about it. Strangely enough, it's not that work-life balance in general is frowned upon; it's specifically not acceptable for women to prioritize their families. Men tend to get praised for putting home first . . ." Kim trailed off, aware that what she was saying could be tough for Patrick to hear.

"Wow. That is disturbing," Patrick responded. Looking up, he spied the tow truck arriving to assist with his flat tire. With a rueful laugh, he observed, "Saved by the tow truck, at least for the moment. Seriously, Kim, thank you for your candor. I've been unhappy recently, as you noticed, and you've given me a lot to think about. Surprisingly, I feel better to have more clarity about this one issue anyway. You've helped me see how I might begin to approach it. Now I need to get this tire fixed. Thank you for waiting with me and for being so open. Are you up for another conversation once I put my thoughts together?"

"I'd like that, Patrick. It's good for me to see the bigger picture that impacts our success. And I always enjoy you, and being a part of enhancing our culture. Count me in." Kim waved and headed for her car as Patrick turned to greet the tow truck driver. Despite the hassle of a flat tire and the worrisome concerns he and Kim had discussed, Patrick noted that he was feeling strangely better than he had in quite a while.

9

LYNN LONGS FOR STABILITY

The next morning found Jack and Lynn heading out the door for their peer coaching meeting. As they began to walk, Lynn launched in. "Volatility means explosive. That's what VUCA is, Jack. We just can't risk that. It could all blow up in our faces. Any risks we face must be immediately dealt with. I know Donna has been good at branding and business development in the past, but I don't think she's doing her job right now. She's dug a hole for all of us. And I don't think she is right about ignoring the risks of VUCA to just focus on our vision for the future. We have to deal with these dangers as soon as possible. I don't understand how Donna can think that clarifying our vision is adequate for addressing the situation we are in. You saw the article in *Tech Consulting Review*, Jack. It's bad news that we've been highlighted in a prominent publication in such a negative light."

"I don't think we have the choice to change something that's already been published, Lynn. You and Arun both agree that we don't have a libel case to make against *Tech Consulting Review*. And Donna is not the only one who should have a pulse on our reputation. That's a responsibility all of us have. As far as volatility goes, it exists, whether we like it or not. We don't get to choose. The question is: What do we do about it?" Gently, he added, "And it's not a matter of you being right and Donna being wrong, or the other way around. You are both smart. You are both experts in your fields. How can we leverage the best of both of you in this situation?"

The two walked on in silence for a few minutes. Finally, Lynn spoke again. "Jack, it's not natural for me to tolerate a situation and just wait to see how things turn out. I need to be doing something. What can I do?"

"That's a good question, Lynn. What have you considered?"

"I've ruled out a suit against the magazine, but I haven't ruled out contacting them to understand the basis of their contention that we are on a downslide. I suppose that could be helpful to us. I know it was Arun's first question," Lynn said thoughtfully.

Lynn sounded more determined as she continued, "We have other risks besides bad press. One of the techies who left us recently has ignored our noncompete clause and taken two of our smaller clients. I need to contact him and let them know we plan to enforce the reimbursement provision. He owes us 20% of fees collected from those clients for the next two years, and of course can't use any of the proprietary products we've created. That's something I can address today."

"Okay. And that is some small support for the revenue vision we came up with yesterday. We won't lose all that money. What else can you do?" Jack pressed.

"I guess I could speak to Patrick," Lynn offered.

Jack was perplexed. "What would you talk with him about?"

"Well, we said we want engaged employees, and I do see disengagement as a risk to our company. We aren't getting the best out of team members if they aren't engaged. Maybe Patrick and I could come up with something that would help." Lynn seemed uncertain again, but went on. "I'm outside of my comfort zone here, Jack, and I don't like it. Still, I don't see any way to create more growth and stability for Tech Environments without focusing on its people. Patrick and I are very different in our perspectives; maybe we would make a good team."

Having made a full circuit of walking the Tech Environments campus, Jack and Lynn had arrived back at their starting point. "Another trip around, Lynn?" Jack inquired.

"No, Jack, but thanks. I have things to do." Smiling for the first time that morning, Lynn hurried off toward her office.

Jack watched Lynn go before turning back into his building. *Maybe this won't turn out to be completely bad,* he thought. *I wonder if having a fire lit under us could end up being useful, even if it is uncomfortable.*

10

EDGAR VISITS FOR
OLD TIME'S SAKE

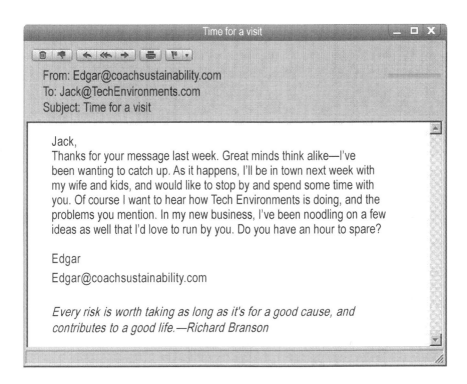

Jack,

Thanks for your message last week. Great minds think alike—I've been wanting to catch up. As it happens, I'll be in town next week with my wife and kids, and would like to stop by and spend some time with you. Of course I want to hear how Tech Environments is doing, and the problems you mention. In my new business, I've been noodling on a few ideas as well that I'd love to run by you. Do you have an hour to spare?

Edgar

Edgar@coachsustainability.com

Every risk is worth taking as long as it's for a good cause, and contributes to a good life.—Richard Branson

With the team's recent conversations about risk, Jack had often thought about Edgar, the Chief Risk Officer who Lynn had replaced. Edgar had left Tech Environments three years earlier when he discovered his son was being bullied at his middle school. The family had moved to a town several hundred miles away. Jack had recently reached out just to see how Edgar was doing, and had been pleased to get a quick response to his email message.

Responding to Edgar's message had been a no-brainer. Jack was eager to reconnect.

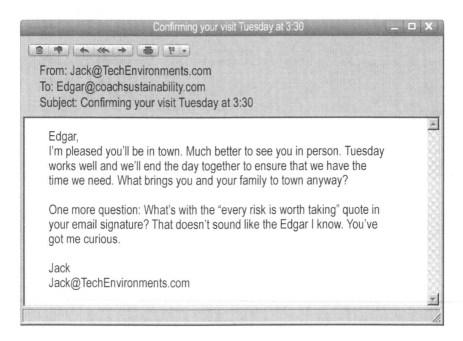

It was Tuesday at 3:30 p.m. when Edgar tapped on Jack's door frame. Grinning, Jack got up and gave him an enthusiastic handshake, "It's so good to see you, Edgar. I can't believe it's been almost three years since you left us. I've heard good things from your clients about what you've been doing for them with your new venture. Just wish you weren't over two hundred miles away."

"It's great to see you, Jack. How's your new Chief Risk Officer doing? You know how bad I felt leaving TE so soon after taking on that role," Edgar finished guiltily.

Jack reassured his friend. "Lynn is a really good CRO, Edgar. There's some friction between her and our Chief Marketing Officer right now, but as far as the risk management program, Lynn picked up right where you left off. She is doing a great job. However, the environment is becoming more challenging every day. And Lynn is struggling as much as any other risk management specialist. Even the big guys like health care companies and credit rating bureaus are getting hacked these days, and of course there are countless other risks too—economic woes, bad press, disgruntled former employees. We've had our fair share recently. Lynn is very proactive, and a good communicator. She helps us manage our risks even though we can't get rid of them entirely."

Edgar smiled. "Your confidence in your new Chief Risk Officer relieves my guilt, Jack. But it also confuses me—you said you had a big problem you wanted to talk with me about today?"

No longer smiling, Jack nodded. "It's the biggest risk we've ever faced as a company, Edgar. The senior leadership team had been functioning fairly well as a team, thanks to some of the soul searching and team development work we did with Jordan a few years back. However, we seem to be stuck on how to respond to the current set of challenges. Just last week, we finally discovered the name for the phenomenon we are experiencing—something called VUCA. It stands for Volatility, Uncertainty, Complexity, and Ambiguity. That's it in a nutshell—we are dealing with all those issues. At least now we have a diagnosis for what's wrong. Is VUCA anything you've run across in your consulting?"

Now it was Edgar's turn to grin. "All the time, Jack, all the time. In a way, VUCA is what I've built my one-man consulting operation on. If you want to know the truth, every company that hires me has one or several of those problems—rapid ups and downs, uncertainty, too many different moving pieces and priorities, a lack of clarity. It's frequently the first step I take in a business engagement—talking about the concepts of VUCA and helping leaders to name them. Once clients get a handle on what they are dealing with, it's easier to begin to recognize what to do about it. Often, as you observed, it's reassuring just to recognize that your company is not alone."

Jack nodded thoughtfully, but said nothing, so Edgar continued. "I've been noticing that VUCA comes up at home too. You remember the reason I left here a few years ago?"

"Of course," Jack agreed. "Having a son get bullied to the point of swallowing pills to hurt himself is something no dad could ever forget. How is Josh doing now?"

"He's great, actually, really healthy and happy again. But speaking of VUCA and constant change, Josh threw us a curveball recently. He wants to move back here, to our old hometown, for high school. He is confident that he understands how to contend with bullies now, and his counselor agrees. Now that Josh is done with middle school, and our daughter is getting ready to start, it seems like the ideal time to move. In my mind, that brings up a couple of the aspects of VUCA—uncertainty and complexity, at least. It would be simpler and more predictable if we stayed put. My business is on solid ground, and our home is in a great school district. However, in addition to Josh asking to move back, my wife Bobbie has never stopped missing her friends here. Regardless of how hard it might be, I believe that family comes first. I am game to make the move."

Jack now looked uneasy. "Edgar, we'd love to have you back. You know that. But Lynn has been here for a couple of years now, and she's done a really good job in your old role. I'm not sure what to say."

"Whoa, Jack, hold on! You misunderstood. I'm not here to ask you for my old job back. I'm enjoying my consulting gigs and my flexibility too much to be an employee again. And I'm plenty busy—as you said, there is no shortage of work for someone who helps companies manage their risks. I do have a proposal for you, but it's not asking you to get rid of Lynn and put me back in my old role."

Jack breathed a visible sigh of relief. "In that case, I'm all ears, Edgar. What do you have in mind?"

11

DO WE NEED A DIFFERENT KIND OF HELP?

The rainy day had everyone on the SLT shaking out umbrellas and raincoats, then filling their coffee cups as they prepared for the start of their meeting. The screen at the front of the room displayed the six envisioned results they'd identified at their previous meeting. Each now included a one-word lead-in to capture the gist of the aspiration.

1. Values: A set of clear and relevant values that give us a road map to work and live by
2. Engagement: An engaged team of associates who see themselves as problem solvers and want to be here
3. Innovation: An updated and expanded set of products and methodologies to offer our clients
4. Leadership: Leaders who are role models for the values we espouse
5. Revenues: Robust revenues that enable confidence and growth
6. Reputation: Positive visibility in the press regarding our culture and our positive impact for our clients and community[5]

"It's hard to believe our off-site was just a week ago," Jack began the SLT meeting. "We left there agreeing to look at the existing bright spots in realizing our desired vision. In the meanwhile, I heard from at least one of you that focusing only on outcomes and not the threat felt risky. Coincidentally, I also heard back from Edgar, who used to be here at Tech Environments as our Chief Risk Officer. He's in town for a few days with his family, and I've invited Edgar in to our SLT meeting today to add his perspective on VUCA. Edgar is going to share his insights about how we might move forward."

Edgar greeted everyone and pulled up a chair to the table. "Great to see you all again! And to hear about the great work you've been doing, Lynn. Jack says you have filled my shoes here, and then some."

Lynn beamed, and leaned back in her chair.

"It's good to see you again, Edgar," Patrick said.

"I heard rumors you might be moving back," Donna remarked.

"Glad to hear that Josh is doing so well!" Ted nodded to his former colleague.

Edgar smiled at their comments before standing up and passing around a stack of one-pagers to the members of the senior leadership team. "It's a little strange to be back here with you all, and yet not be a member of the team," Edgar began. "It's even stranger to be telling you I think you need me and that you should hire me. Jack and I met yesterday, and we both agree that it has to be a team decision."

Everyone around the table appeared engaged, and Edgar went on. "Jack has informed me that you've been struggling with VUCA. I know VUCA very well myself. It feels overwhelming and unsustainable, and we are all facing it. As I believe you all know, when I left Tech Environments and moved away, I started a consulting business in my new hometown. When I launched the company, I expected to be helping companies to manage risk. However, I recently rebranded as a sustainability consultant. I've spent the past couple of years studying up on how companies, the military, and even individuals are dealing with the feverish rate of change we are experiencing today, also known as VUCA. I've been doing some fractional work as a Chief Sustainability Officer for a few midsized companies, and we are getting some positive results."

Donna interrupted Edgar. "Hold on a minute, Edgar. I'm not sure I follow you. I understood sustainability was about environmental hazards and recycling. I assumed it was mostly compliance issues. What does sustainability have to do with the change we are experiencing, or with VUCA, for that matter?"

"You're right, Donna. 'Sustainability,'" Edgar gestured with air quotes, "used to be limited to a focus on the environment—water, air, land, energy, natural resources. The business context for sustainability has become much broader than that now.[6] As a sustainability consultant, I help companies to make thoughtful decisions that will enable them to thrive for the long term. That is, to be sustainable. The work sometimes includes reducing their negative impact on the environment, but 'environment' (again, Edgar used air quotes) includes not just the natural environment but the organization's culture, the broader community, the industry you are in, employees' families, and society as a whole. The longer I do this work, the more I find that sustainability is a more significant issue than just the physical environment. Sustainable success requires that you maximize leadership capacity and employee retention, as well as developing robust policies and procedures, effective strategy, and resource conservation and renewal. Those are all sustainability issues. I could go on and on. These are the critical factors that affect employee engagement and business results. And VUCA is a constant threat to sustainability." Edgar paused before adding, "I apologize for the mini-lecture. As you can see, I am passionate about the work I do."

"So what are you saying, Edgar?" Arun had been uncharacteristically quiet, but now interrupted. "What can you do that we haven't already got a consultant doing, or someone who's right in this room?" He glanced quickly at Lynn.

Edgar remembered Arun's bluntness and wasn't offended by the direct question. "How's that working for you, Arun?" he asked quietly.

"Exactly!" exclaimed Jack. "Lynn is doing her job well and has accomplished a great deal. But this is a new challenge that we don't have experience with. I believe we could use Edgar's help."

Ted cleared his throat. "I'm sorry to disagree, Jack. I admire Edgar too, but there's no way we should incur additional expenses at this point. According to the last numbers I ran, expenses are running significantly ahead of budget and our revenues are well behind. The finance team is looking at where we can reduce expenses. We are definitively not looking to add to our costs at this lean time. Hiring another consultant is not an option."

Patrick was the only one at the table who wasn't nodding in agreement with the CFO's assertion. Instead, he was scanning the document Edgar had handed out as they got started. "Hold on just a minute," he said. "Check this out—we haven't even given Edgar a chance to share the bottom-line cost yet. He's offering us two months of his sustainability consulting services for free. It's not just a money-back guarantee, folks. It's a guarantee that there's no money out the door unless he proves the value of what he's offering."

Ted looked at Edgar with friendly concern. "Do you think that's a good idea, Edgar? Can you really afford not to bill us when you are anticipating a costly move with your family?"

"Strangely enough, I can." Edgar responded calmly. "As you'll see, I think I've identified the keys to sustainability, and that applies for my own business and my family's well-being just the way it applies to Tech Environments. I'm convinced that if you'll provide me with your time and let me work with your team, I can be of help. If what I've seen at other firms is any indication, you'll experience both increased revenue generation and cost savings. By the end of two months, I expect that Ted will be telling this team that you can't afford NOT to hire me."

Surprised by Edgar's conviction, Jack commented, "You've certainly grown in confidence since you left here, Edgar. You make it sound like you have some of the answers we need. And I certainly can't think of a downside now that you've taken cost off the table. What does everyone else think?"

"I'm in," Lynn said quickly.

"Me too," echoed Ted and Donna.

"Can't see any reason why not," Arun grudgingly agreed.

"So long as Edgar includes all of us, and brings Jordan up to speed for how she can help, and assuming we don't make things too complicated, I'm all for it!" Patrick made it unanimous.

Giving Edgar the thumbs-up sign, Jack smiled warmly at his former employee. "Looks like you are on the team, Edgar. I hope that these next two months enable you to make us all believers. Maybe you'll be able to share some of the bright spots you see as well as shedding light on VUCA and our challenges."

12

ARUN WRESTLES
WITH UNCERTAINTY

It had been a while since Jordan had met with Arun for individual coaching, so she'd been surprised when he'd reached out the previous day to request a coaching session. Jordan's long-term relationship with Tech Environments had been a rock-solid one over the years. TE continued to pay her a retainer each month for the inevitable coaching needs that arose for teams and for individual leaders at the firm. So Jordan wasn't surprised to get a request from Tech Environments, just startled that the call had come from Arun. Of all the leaders at the company, Arun tended to be the most self-assured. But here he was in her office, and at the moment he appeared far from confident.

"As you know, I tend to believe I'm right," Arun opened the conversation before he was even fully seated in the comfortable chair Jordan offered him. "I know what I want, and I tend to execute quickly when I'm sure of something."

Jordan nodded to Arun to continue.

"To be honest, even if I'm wrong, I'd rather be moving than standing still," he admitted.

Smiling, Jordan commented, "Sounds like there might be a 'but' coming?"

Arun, unaccustomed to feeling unsure, stared down at his hands. "But the situation we have now at Tech Environments is different from any I've faced before. I've always been able to trust myself. In the past, I've invariably come through with a solution when our company has experienced obstacles. But it seems that I might not have all the answers anymore. And Jack is not a fan of me at the moment, which doesn't help."

Jordan waited, as Arun seemed to be wrestling with what he wanted to say.

He blurted, "What if I'm not innovative enough to propel Tech Environments into the future? I'm sure Jack blames me for our weak product pipeline, revenue shortfalls, and for misreading our clients. He talks about 'the next version of Tech Environments,' and he wants it now, not later. I don't even understand what he's talking about. I've been sure for a while I can't keep playing both the role of Chief Operating Officer and Chief Technical Officer. That's one thing I am sure of. I can't tolerate doing both positions only halfway well. And it's clear to me that Jack won't stand for that either. I'd say in his current mindset, he's not likely to give me much time to create some momentum." Arun sat back in his seat, staring down at his hands. "I'm not sure what to do."

Jordan spoke quietly, "Arun, as unclear as your situation is, it strikes me that there is a great deal you *are* sure of. You just mentioned several things you're positive about. Would it be helpful to list some of those?"

Arun smiled slightly, the first sign of optimism he'd shown since arriving in her office. "That would be a relief. I've been struggling with this for several weeks now, and I'm not sure I've gotten any clearer in my thinking. Our recent SLT meetings haven't made it any better."

"Okay, so what is already evident to you?" Jordan had grabbed a marker and was prepared to jot down what Arun shared on the whiteboard mounted on her office wall.

"I'm sure that Jack is expecting more of me, that he is impatient." Jordan captured his comment.

"It's obvious that I'm getting burned out playing two leadership roles; I'm exhausted and not sleeping well. I've dropped some balls with monitoring our client portfolio. I'm not available to my team when they need me. And I'm positive that at least a couple of my project team managers are interviewing at other companies."

Jordan noted these on the list they were creating before asking, "What else?"

1. Jack's high expectations and impatience
2. Feeling burned out and exhausted
3. Dropping balls, like monitoring and balancing client portfolio
4. Unavailable to team
5. PMs interviewing at other companies

Arun examined the list. "I guess we should add that Edgar is back, and that he seems to have Jack's confidence, certainly more than I do. I'm not sure what else. Is there anything else you heard me say?"

Jordan considered Arun's observation, pausing for a moment before offering, "It sounds as if you believe that the consulting environment is different than it's ever been before, that your clients are expecting more of you?"

Arun agreed, "Yes, that's true. The customers are wanting a one-stop shop for their needs. They want the efficiency of dealing with fewer vendors, and still expect us to be best in class."

Jordan added the last items to the list. Then she waited as Arun reviewed what she'd summarized.

1. Jack's high expectations and impatience
2. Feeling burned out and exhausted
3. Dropping balls, like monitoring and balancing client portfolio
4. Unavailable to team
5. PMs interviewing at other companies
6. Edgar back in new leadership consulting role
7. Technology consulting environment has changed

When he'd finished evaluating the list, Arun voiced his agreement, "That's it exactly. Jack has lost confidence in me. My direct reports have lost confidence in me. Our clients have lost confidence in us. And I'm a mess. I think that pretty well captures it. It's funny that even though it looks like an overwhelming list, it's better just to have it all written down. At least I'm sure of some things, even if they aren't good," he observed.

"Yes, you seem calmer than when you walked in," Jordan responded. "So what's next? What do you want to take action on?"

Arun answered quickly, "I guess I need to talk to Edgar. He's had diverse experiences with other companies and has a desire to create sustainable results. I'm confident it will be useful to meet with him. Honestly, I've been viewing Edgar as competition instead of as a resource."

"That sounds like a plan, Arun. When will you meet with Edgar?"

Pulling out his iPhone, Arun quickly texted a message before looking up at Jordan with a slight grin. "Just sent him a request. You know me—I like action once I'm sure about something. I'll let you know how it turns out." Arun got up and reached out to shake Jordan's hand. "Thanks, Jordan. I appreciate that you helped me think this through. Once I admit I need an objective partner, coaching always seems worthwhile. You are very practical in the help you offer, and I'm grateful."

Shaking Arun's hand, Jordan nodded at his heartfelt appreciation. "My pleasure, Arun. I look forward to hearing how it goes with Edgar."

13

NOW YOU?

Jack tossed the phone on his desk, disheartened by the call he'd just ended. *You'd think my wife would know my company is in a crisis. Sure, our daughter's college graduation is important, but it's still weeks away. Why bother me about that now? She knows I can't commit to going, not unless something dramatic happens here. And now pushing to go down early for us to have some time together? Geez, it's more likely she'll just have to go by herself!*

Ted tapped on Jack's door. "Got a second?" Seeing the expression on Jack's face, Ted backed up quickly. "Never mind, it can wait."

"You're already here, so go ahead," Jack instructed Ted.

"I think my timing is off, Jack. I'll come back tomorrow when you are having a better day."

"Oh come on, Ted! Why are you here? You've already interrupted me, so tell me what you wanted!" Though not raising his voice, it was clear Jack was irritated.

Ted carefully pulled the door shut behind him as he entered the office. As the longest-serving leader on Tech Environments' SLT, Ted was accustomed to Jack's strong emotions and high expectations of himself. He realized that, with the company struggling, Jack himself was struggling to stay calm and centered. When possible, Ted chose to postpone talking to Jack about anything when the CEO was in this state of mind. But . . . *I'm not sure delay is an option right now*, Ted thought. *I guess my best choice is to continue with what I was going to say.*

Ted decided to be direct. "Take a breath, Jack, and let's sit down. I have an issue I need your help with." When Jack had taken a seat, Ted went on, "You know Jen, the newest member of my team?" Jack nodded, and Ted continued. "Jen is smart. She's motivated. She works hard. Jen is an asset to Tech Environments."

"Sounds all good. What's the problem?" Jack asked.

Ted responded without hesitation to his boss's question. "It's you."

"Huh? What are you talking about?" Jack exclaimed.

"Jen is talented and she's courageous, Jack. She's not afraid to take risks or be wrong, so long as she is learning. In fact, I haven't run across a single thing that Jen is afraid of. However, she IS afraid of Arun. Her impression is that he's always mad at her, never satisfied with her performance. He's blunt, unappreciative, and closed to others' perspectives. Jen has no idea what she is doing wrong, and that's not good. She's worried that she's failing. Fortunately, she trusts me enough to come and ask what she can change to make it better. Frankly, Jack, it's not Jen who needs to change. It's you." Ted looked directly at Jack. "You've let Arun get away with this behavior for entirely too long. He's a bully, and regardless of how technically strong he is, it's an issue you need to address."

Jack looked stunned by Ted's declaration. *Today is going from bad to worse. My wife is already mad at me, and now my CFO. What next?*

Taking one last look to be sure Jack had understood what he was saying, Ted finished, "I'll show myself out, Jack. Let me know when you'd like to talk." And Ted left Jack to his own reflections.

14

NO LONGER
HORSING AROUND

Jack was stuck. *Something has to change. I feel like I'm losing my company and my family. But I have no idea where to start. What was it Jordan told me about when we talked? Horses?* Jack remembered a conversation with Coach Jordan where she had told him about coaches who used horses to develop leaders. *What was it she called it? Oh yeah, equine coaching.*[7] At the time, Jack had thought Jordan was off base. He couldn't imagine what horses had to do with leadership. After his awful conversation with Ted, however, Jack was willing to try anything.

Searching in his desk drawer, Jack quickly located the business card and made the call. "Hi, we haven't met, but I'm Jack, CEO of Tech Environments. Our coach Jordan has recommended you, and I'm in a bind. I wonder if you'd be willing to meet with me?"

Jack was relieved when Marge was able to fit him in quickly. As he drove toward the horse farm the next morning, he found himself going back and forth—hopeful one moment and skeptical the next. *What could a horse have to teach me? Why didn't Jordan just tell me what I need to do?* As he arrived at the farm, Jack pulled up to the fence and took a deep breath before exiting his car.

"You must be Jack," said a woman decked out in cowboy boots and jeans. "I'm Marge. It's good to meet you." As they shook hands, Marge continued, "You mentioned on the phone that you wanted to sort out something." She gestured toward the barn. "Let me introduce you to Ellie. She's the horse you'll be working with today. If anyone can help you work something out for yourself, it's Ellie."

Three hours in to being in the ring with Ellie, Jack felt an appreciation of his problem that he hadn't experienced before. *My wife, kids, and Tech Environments' colleagues have all given me plenty of feedback, but it just hasn't stuck.* He recalled that he would improve for a while—take care of himself, spend time with his family, not take himself so damn seriously. And on those days, Jack enjoyed his job and life all over again. But it never seemed to last. Recently, he'd been tired and impatient, worrying about his marriage and his company. Jack recognized he hadn't been taking care of things that mattered, like Arun's behavior toward others. He just wanted to be in control again. He wanted to feel he had a handle on how to turn his company around. He had been embarrassed by his irritability with his wife and with Ted; they weren't to blame. However, his attempts to rein himself in and breathe had no staying power. When worry got the best of him, Jack did what Jack did, and as a result nothing got solved, and he was even more anxious.

Because, he recognized, *I believe I'm the only one who can fix what's wrong. And,* he admitted to himself, *because getting exasperated usually works well for me. Everyone backs off with their demands, or moves into action when they sense I'm upset. I guess the question now is: Who do I really want to be? I've always been self-sufficient, feeling like I should be the one in control. Even if I wanted to, can I really change something about myself that has been there as long as I can remember?*

Today, his attempts at control hadn't worked at all well with Ellie. In fact, the mare had basically ignored Jack when he came into the ring insistent that she follow him. It didn't matter to the horse that Jack was aggravated when she didn't comply. Ellie had calmly walked away from him, to the other side of the fenced enclosure. Even when he followed her and grabbed Ellie's halter to lead her in the direction he wanted, Jack found that moving a 1200-pound mare required her cooperation. Regardless of how irked he became, he couldn't force Ellie to move without finding a way to communicate with her, and then getting her cooperation. Jack had to get himself under control. He was obliged to respect Ellie before he could accomplish anything.

The equine coach Marge had been alternately supportive and challenging as Jack kept doing things the way he'd always done them. By the end of the morning, though, Jack had experienced a shift—in himself, and in his ability to truly engage with the horse. He'd begun to have fun, and Ellie had responded. She seemed to enjoy him too when he wasn't trying to control her. *Becoming partners with someone who outweighs me six-fold,* he considered. *That's big.*

And maybe that's what Tech Environments has become too, Jack thought as he drove home. *Big. The company has become too much for me to move single-handedly. I don't have a choice but to find a new way. VUCA is not going away, and nothing in my power can make that happen. As Jordan has told me, I need to become a different kind of leader for this VUCA world. I can still be Jack, but a new and expanded version of me. If I don't demonstrate the capacity to adapt and flex to the situation, I can't be the sort of leader I was in the ring with Ellie. A good leader listens. He shows care and consideration. I have to recognize that I'm not in this alone. That's not going to be easy. Guess there's nothing like starting now.*

As he drove, Jack pressed the hands-free calling feature on his steering wheel. He said aloud, "Phone Jordan."

"Calling Coach Jordan," the mechanical voice responded. Jack smiled as he heard the phone ringing at the other end. His smile quickly turned to a frown when Jordan's voice mail picked up. Swallowing his disappointment at having to wait before speaking with her, Jack dictated a message on her voice mail. "Jordan, this is Jack. Turns out it was a good idea you had to send me to the equine coach. I learned a lot, and managed to escape without the horse crushing me, though I'm sure she wanted to. I've got a lot of work to do, and I'm confident about the impact if I commit to making a change. I'd appreciate your support on this one. Can you and I get some time on our schedules for coaching?"

Pressing the call complete button, Jack headed for home, humming. *I don't have any illusions that it is going to be easy, but I'm glad to finally have a clue about what and who I want to be. And that needs to start at home. I have an apology to make, and some trip planning to do with my wife. Graduations and time together don't come around often enough; I need to make sure I'm focusing on what's most important.*

15

STRUGGLING TO FIND CLARITY

Ted sat down with Raj on the patio just outside his office building.

"I know you probably thought it was strange to get a call from the CFO," Ted began. "But I've heard a lot about how much you are into neuroscience, and I have the idea that you might be able to help me, actually to assist all of us. You've developed quite a reputation around here as a leader who has transformed himself. And I've heard Patrick and several others say that the key for you has been understanding the neuroscience behind the way our brains work."

Raj smiled and nodded, waiting for Ted to continue.

"Raj, you also have a reputation for being able to preserve a confidence, so I'd like to be sure that what we talk about today is something you are willing to keep to yourself. Can I have your word on that?"

Once again Raj nodded and patiently waited for Ted to get to the point.

"Thanks. Here's the issue—what I've noticed is that when our insecurity gets sparked, we get the worst version of everyone on the senior leadership team. You've probably seen, or heard about, some of what I'm talking about. Arun gets anxious that he's behind on technology, so he berates his team. Patrick worries about the engagement scores or Glassdoor reviews and stops playing the role of team mediator. Lynn gets completely risk-averse and puts obstacles in the way of every initiative, not to mention attacking others when she feels they have created avoidable risks. Jack becomes controlling and reverts to trusting only himself, so he becomes a bottleneck. Donna's travel budget goes through the roof as she advertises more and puts all our sales reps on the road. She also talks incessantly, which irritates us all no end." Ted stopped to take a breath.

Ted sighed. "I'm sure I am at my worst too, Raj. I know that I tighten the purse strings, resisting expenditures even when they make sense. Certainly, my wife is not happy with my mood when I'm home." Ted glanced over at Raj to see his reaction.

"So you've witnessed what happens when the senior leadership team is stressed," Raj acknowledged Ted's observations. "I suspect that you are wondering—now that you see the problem—what can you do to become effective again? And, since you came to me, I am guessing that you think there is a neuroscience explanation for what is happening. If that's what you were hoping, Ted, you came to the right place." Now Raj smiled broadly, clearly enjoying himself. "You need to pause when you get triggered."

"Remind me about being triggered?" Ted was confused.

Raj nodded, "Sure. Triggered is when something really gets under your skin, and others get the worst version of you. Literally. Once your amygdala gets triggered, or hijacked, it takes about 17 minutes before you regain access to the reasonable, thoughtful, collaborative, creative part of your brain. One way to avoid being offline for that period of time, Ted, is to get better at pausing. Or you could try to avoid being triggered in the first place. From what you are telling me, the whole senior leadership team needs to learn that."[8]

"You make it sound easy, Raj. I suspect it's harder than I think," Ted acknowledged. "Where do we start?"

16

WE NEED TO DO SOMETHING ABOUT THE DRAMA

The air in this conference room feels frigid, but maybe that is just my imagination. Donna was seated at the conference table. She gestured to Lynn to sit down, waiting impatiently as Lynn walked all the way around the table to seat herself some distance away. Donna tossed two slim blue paperbacks onto the conference room table.

"What's this?" Lynn asked. She picked up the book and read its cover, shaking her head in confusion. "The Power of TED*?"[9]

"It's something I'd like the two of us to read. And then I'd like us to live it," Donna responded. "There is entirely too much drama between us."

Lynn bristled, "That's odd coming from you. It sounds like a sexist remark, seeing drama between the only two women on the senior leadership team. I'd have expected better from you."

"I'm not being sexist, Lynn. It's reality. There's been friction between the two of us for as long as we've worked together. I get it—we have different styles. You like structure and detail," Donna gestured toward Lynn. "And I like flexibility and focusing on the big picture. You're quiet and reflective," again she pointed at Lynn. "And I'm extroverted and

63

talkative. Those attributes are what I most appreciate about each of us, why I am glad we are both on this team. However, our destructive skirmishes, our animosity toward each other, have got to stop."

Lynn interrupted. "You and I might not get along, but that doesn't get in my way of doing my job, or anyone else doing theirs."

"I disagree," Donna countered. "You think just because we don't yell that no one feels the tension, that it's not conflict. What I am just beginning to recognize is how much it does affect others. Have you not noticed that the two of us are never on the same task forces, seldom in the same meetings? People around here go through great gyrations trying to ensure that the two of us are not in the room at the same time. It saps energy, wastes time, and it hurts our results. Maybe reading this TED* book will get you and me back on the right track." Donna maintained her gaze on Lynn, as if daring her to argue.

Lynn, who'd been paging through the book while Donna was talking, now commented. "The Power of TED*. The Empowerment Dynamic," she read again from the cover. "Are you telling me this is one more extra thing I need to do because you can be hard to get along with?" She shrugged, "Oh well, it looks like an easy read anyway. You'll probably get it read while you are jet-setting around the country."

Donna objected, "That's exactly what I mean, Lynn. You and I often get in a dig at one another wherever we can. It's unnecessary."

Lynn glared at Donna, then shrugged. "I admit you have a point, Donna. We've both worked hard to get to where we are, and our feuding distracts us from what really matters." Lynn paused. "Will you at least acknowledge that men do drama too?"

"No doubt," Donna grinned. "I got the book from Patrick, who gave it to me when I told him I was looking for a resource for us. He is taking the online course for a deeper dive to help him practice this way of thinking. I'm hopeful that it will make a big difference for us."

"I had no idea what you wanted to meet about, Donna. I'm not sure that this will work, but I'm willing to read the book if you will." Lynn picked up her copy. "Hopefully, we'll be able to figure things out from there."

17

VALUES TO RECONNECT WITH IN TIMES OF CHANGE

Edgar had no idea if his exercise to generate Tech Environments' new company values would work. *I know involving everyone is the best way to make sure they all buy in*, he reflected. *But will there be any clear winners? And will Jack and the senior leadership team buy in if their preferred values aren't the ones that emerge?*

Edgar reviewed the company-wide email he was getting ready to send out.

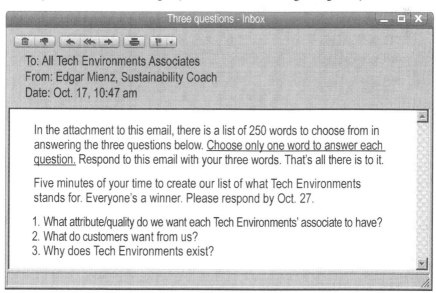

Three questions - Inbox

To: All Tech Environments Associates
From: Edgar Mienz, Sustainability Coach
Date: Oct. 17, 10:47 am

In the attachment to this email, there is a list of 250 words to choose from in answering the three questions below. <u>Choose only one word to answer each question.</u> Respond to this email with your three words. That's all there is to it.

Five minutes of your time to create our list of what Tech Environments stands for. Everyone's a winner. Please respond by Oct. 27.

1. What attribute/quality do we want each Tech Environments' associate to have?
2. What do customers want from us?
3. Why does Tech Environments exist?

Edgar took one last look before he clicked "send to all" and leaned back in his chair. *We won't get sustainability if we can't be succinct. And we won't get there without engagement from everyone. Here goes nothing.*

Five days later, Edgar had his answer. At least he was relatively sure he had it. He'd received responses from over 80% of Tech Environments' associates—an impressive response rate—and he'd done the simplest thing he could to combine their responses. Including all the words that at least 20% of TE's associates had sent, Edgar had used a word cloud app to create a picture of sorts. The results seemed obvious to him. Would others see it the same way? Exhaling, Edgar printed out seven copies of the word cloud image to take to the SLT meeting. He put one in front of each place at the conference room table, and then sat down to wait.

The senior leadership team members were all gazing at the handout as they got settled into their seats. Some turned the word cloud around to look at it from different angles. Others left the sheet in front of them on the table, appearing to examine it.

"Well?" Edgar finally asked. "What do you all think?"

"They are all powerful words, undeniably important in our culture," Ted commented.

"Looks clear to me," Arun declared. "Integrity. Innovation. Impact. Those are our values. Thanks, Edgar. This is solid."

"Integrity, Innovation, Impact," concurred Donna. "I like it—three I's. If we live those three values, it's going to make us sustainable. Great work."

Lynn and Patrick both smiled and nodded. "I think the team will find it inspiring," Patrick commented.

Jack spoke ruefully, "It seems obvious now that we have it. We must have integrity—that's core to who we are. If we have integrity, the level of trust will be high and everyone will be engaged and creative—we will be innovative. And we know that TE being able to innovate is key to our impact for our clients and industry. Yes, I can see that this will offer a strong foundation for what we stand for well into the future." Jack gave Edgar the thumbs-up.

Edgar gazed around at his colleagues and smiled. *Nothing like a clear win to make a consultant feel good,* he thought. *Now let's see what we do with this.*

18

ARUN FEELS THE HEAT

Despite the cool day, Arun was sure he was sweating as he headed for his meeting with Jack and Patrick. The meeting had been added to Arun's calendar two days earlier, simply labeled as "Meeting with Patrick and Jack." It was scheduled in Patrick's office, which suggested it was at his initiation, but Patrick hadn't shared any details with Arun, despite their being paired as peer coaches. *Something about this does not bode well for me,* Arun thought. *Oh well, might as well get it over with, whatever it is.*

Jack and Patrick were already seated when Arun arrived. *Another bad sign,* he thought. The serious expressions on their faces validated his concern. Feigning confidence, Arun asked brusquely, "What's up? I didn't see an agenda attached to the meeting invite."

Patrick and Jack glanced at one another before Jack took the lead. "Arun, we have something somewhat sensitive that we wanted to discuss, and didn't want you to come into the meeting feeling defensive—so felt it would be better for you to just come in 'cold.' We are committed to supporting you. However, it's important that you know that the way things are going cannot continue. I suspect that you have at least some idea of why Patrick and I scheduled this meeting. Let's start there—what are you already aware of that we need to talk about?"

Arun could feel the heat spread up his cheeks. "I would like to think it's about how to be more innovative in our approach to new business. I was happy to see innovation as one of our three core values for the firm. However, I doubt that the two of you would be meeting with me in this way to discuss innovation. So I assume that you've received a complaint about me. Beyond that, I don't know. It's not the first time. Some people are just overly sensitive. You know me. I am abrupt. I am opinionated. I always think I'm right. I certainly don't mean anything by it. You know that."

"Intention is one thing," Patrick sounded serious. "And impact is another. The impact of your behavior is that others feel intimidated, dismissed, and bullied. That creates a hostile work environment, one in which no one can be innovative. People become preoccupied with protecting themselves."

"That's not my intention," insisted Arun. "It's just the way I am. I know some people think I'm arrogant, but I know what I know. Others can know what they know too. They just have to be willing to defend it."

Now Jack joined in. Refusing to allow the meeting to turn into a debate, he asserted, "Arun, we have overlooked your behavior for a very long time now. I have ignored it and let it go. Doing so has done you no favors. You deserve to get feedback; otherwise you can't improve. I've failed you in offering my candid perspective. I'm stepping up now to tell you that your bullying has got to stop. Good people are being hurt by you. That is unacceptable. It always has been—I just wasn't willing to jeopardize our relationship, and perhaps your employment here, by telling you so. There's no question that you bring tremendous value to Tech Environments, that we want you here. However, I can no longer keep you here at any cost. Your strong personality is not the problem—it is your unwillingness to consider the needs of others, and to adapt your leadership style accordingly."

Arun, stiffly upright in his chair, appeared stunned. "I'm not even sure where I would start."

"Start with Jordan," Patrick suggested. "She's known you for several years already, and she is a trustworthy partner. By now, she has assisted nearly all of us on the senior leadership team in one way or another. Her role here is to help us develop ourselves as leaders, and certainly to grow our self-awareness and our effectiveness as a team. Reach out to her, if you are willing, and see whether coaching offers the right approach for you. Jordan will provide other referrals to you if the two of you decide that coaching is not the answer."

Jack brought the meeting to a close. "It's your call, Arun," he stated. "I'm not going to tell you that you have to change, but I am telling you that if there is not a substantial shift in your behavior, you cannot continue here at Tech Environments. Clarifying our values recently makes it apparent that I am out of integrity to allow your behavior, and the negative impact on others, to persist. By year end, there needs to be a measurable difference, or we will work on an exit plan. I have no desire for you to lose face. I know you can succeed, and I hope you do."

Arun looked shaken as he rose from his seat. Not looking at either Jack or Patrick, he left the room.

Patrick regarded Jack after Arun had departed. "Do you think he can do it?"

"I hope so," Jack responded. "I really do think Arun is the one we want leading our technology here. But it's costing us too much to keep him unless he can make a change. Thank you, Patrick, for holding my feet to the fire. This is one thing I never like to do, and something you excel at. I appreciate your leadership." Patting Patrick on the shoulder, Jack left as well.

Did our CEO just say he valued my leadership? Patrick wondered. *It never occurred to me I wasn't just doing my job.*

19

PATRICK WANTS TO "DOUBLE-CLICK"

The Lunch & Learn presentation had attracted a wide array of Tech Environments' associates, and the seats around the U-shaped table setup were nearly all filled. Some of the attendees, if they were being honest, admitted they had just shown up for the free catered lunch. Others came for a chance to connect with friends and colleagues they seldom interacted with in their daily work. And more than a few attended because the topic was something they wanted to learn more about. Today's title—"Double-Clicking to Get on the Same Page: Leadership in a High-Tech World"—was one that sparked curiosity across the organization. Some of Tech Environments' programmers were there, along with senior leaders, support staff, finance team members, and program managers. No one really knew where Patrick might be going with the day's session.

"I guess we should start with the basics," Patrick declared as the session commenced. "What is double-clicking?"

"That's obvious," one woman offered. "It's what you do when you want to open a document on the computer."

"Yeah, either that or just to select a word in a document," someone else offered.

"Good answers," Patrick acknowledged. "What else?"

"If you really want the basics about what it is, double-clicking is pressing your mouse button or key pad twice in quick succession," one of the programmers explained.

"And if you are asking what else it's designed to accomplish," Raj commented, "Double-clicking is often how you launch an application like Excel or Project."

"All your explanations and definitions of double-clicking sound accurate," Patrick agreed. "However, today's Lunch & Learn is a different angle on double-clicking. I'll start with a little background. This take on Double-Clicking is based on work by a social scientist named Judith E. Glaser.[10] Many describe Glaser as an academic and author. Others call her a business executive—she owns a thriving company. Glaser herself often says she is an 'organizational anthropologist,' whatever that is, and a business consultant. In any case, Glaser is definitely not a computer guru, and this session is not about perfecting your computer skills." Patrick waited for the groans from the techies to subside before going on. "Instead, we are going to be talking about how we can improve the quality of our conversations and overcome the blind spots that may prevent us from understanding each other. Anyone want to grab your lunch and escape before we start?" A few around the table looked tempted. Noting the presence of some senior leaders in the room, they stayed in their places. A little visibility never hurt.

Patrick continued, "Conversational blind spots. It's an intriguing term, and as you'll see, a fascinating phenomenon. Conversational blind spots are the times we think we are in dialogue with someone else when in reality we are on completely different tracks. We don't recognize what we are missing as we talk *past* one another, or *at* each other, instead of *with* each other. Has anyone ever had that kind of conversation?"

"Yeah, last week at a client site," admitted Charles. "They kept talking about project plans and deadlines while we were attempting to nail down the overall scope of the project. We both were trying to get what we were there for, and ended up running around in circles."

Patrick responded, "Yes, sometimes the conversational blind spot is that we have two different agendas for the conversation, which makes it hard to accomplish anything. Who else has an example?"

Pete raised his hand and waited to be acknowledged. "I think this happens with my kids sometimes. They get upset about something—not getting enough playing time in soccer, another kid smashing their potato chips at lunch, the unreasonable rules my wife and I have about them doing chores, stuff like that. I tell them it's no big deal; 'this too shall pass.' I don't even listen really because I know in a few days it will be something different. It makes for some pretty unpleasant evenings at our house."

"Good example, Pete. Your kids are talking about something that really matters to them, and rather than seeing it from their perspective, you see it from your own. So you dismiss it as unimportant." Patrick was grateful that participants were sharing so many good examples. He knew that the Lunch & Learn sessions that were interactive were always well-received.

Marianne spoke next. "I have a boss who creates obscure titles for Lunch & Learn sessions. He thinks he's being clever, but people show up expecting a computer skills session instead of learning soft skills like effective conversations." Everyone laughed, knowing that Marianne in her role as Senior Training Manager reported directly to Patrick. Even Patrick seemed to enjoy the humor, not minding being its target.

"In this case, Marianne, I was deliberately ambiguous," Patrick admitted. "Sometimes this crew," he gestured toward the audience, "likes to be surprised. However, you are right that something like a mistitled presentation or email can create a conversational blind spot—the speaker believing that his or her meaning is understood, when in fact it's the listener who determines meaning. Like some of you who came today thinking the only meaning of 'double-click' has to do with computers."

The programmer who'd spoken up earlier interrupted Patrick. "So what is it, then, if it's not computer mouse clicking? What do you mean when you say double-click?"

Patrick gave the programmer a thumbs-up and continued, "Thanks for moving us along. It's a good question. Just as you would double-click on a computer to see what's inside a folder, you can Double-Click in a conversation. Here's how: instead of assuming you know what's inside the other person's head and that you understand what they are saying, you ask a question, or Double-Click, to open that up. With the client Charles mentioned earlier, for example, you could ask, 'What do you mean when you say you want to talk about the project? Can we Double-Click on that so I know exactly what you mean?' In doing so, you gain knowledge about their objective for the conversation. Double-Clicking takes you beyond your assumptions to a shared understanding. Of course, the first step in Double-Clicking is to make sure that others understand that when you ask to Double-Click, you are really saying 'tell me more.'"

"What about the example with my kids?" Pete asked. "I don't want to spend the whole evening listening to their complaints. Does it make any sense to Double-Click in that situation?"

"I think it does, Pete," Patrick responded. "When you Double-Click in a conversation you open up shared understanding and mutual trust. Is it important to you to have your children trust you?"

"You bet!" Pete responded. "If your kids can trust you, they don't keep secrets. If they keep secrets, you can't help them when they have problems."

Patrick acknowledged Pete's contribution, "Yes, you want to be a good parent to your children, and listening to them is key to that. Double-Clicking is one of the best tools I know to promote shared knowledge, and, of course, trust."

Now CTO Arun spoke up, "You mentioned Double-Clicking with clients to get on the same page. Do you think this would have any impact on the success of our client engagements? I mean, we are often bringing our clients technical solutions, and this strikes me as a technical-sounding tool that could actually help us to reduce ambiguity, maybe even in the contracting process."

Patrick agreed enthusiastically. "I appreciate where you are going, Arun. In my experience with Double-Click in conversations so far, one of its most powerful impacts is reducing ambiguity. I've heard you and Charles and many of our consulting team talk about 'scope creep' on your projects, and I think Double-Clicking is a useful tool in minimizing misunderstandings and unexpected changes throughout the client engagement."

Glancing at the clock, Patrick realized time was short. He began to wind up. "Wow, we are almost out of time for this Lunch & Learn session," he announced. "Let me share a resource with you, and then leave you with some homework to add to your individual to-do lists." Laughing, he ignored their moans at the idea of homework and went on, "The resource is Judith E. Glaser's book *Conversational Intelligence*. We have a few of her books available on loan here in our training library if anyone would like to check out a copy. And your homework is easy—try Double-Clicking in a conversation you have in the next week and see what difference it makes. Email your experiences to Marianne, and she'll choose a winner for a $50 gift card to the vendor of your choice."

Patrick enjoyed the round of applause he got for the session, realizing it could be enthusiasm for the contest or genuine appreciation of the session topic. He chatted with a few colleagues as they were leaving. *This is good*, he thought. *It feels like we have a sense of shared goals and understanding, well beyond just Double-Clicking. Maybe Tech Environments really is becoming an Us instead of so many individual contributors. I hope so.* Smiling, he headed out the door and back to his office.

20

KIM REEVALUATES HER VALUES

Kim picked up her phone and chose a name from her contact list. Ever since her conversation with Patrick over his flat tire, Kim had felt reflective. Patrick doubted himself, feeling that he hadn't done his job as well as he should have when it came to managing the Tech Environments culture. While Kim hadn't talked about her own issues to Patrick, the conversation had stayed on her mind. Patrick clearly cared a great deal about his job. *What do I care about at this point in my life?* Kim pondered. *Is TE where I should be? It wasn't easy to come back to work in the first place, and I'm just not sure I'm making a difference. I'm not even sure what difference I hope to make.*

As she heard Raj pick up the phone, Kim started talking immediately, "Hi, Raj. Can I pick your brain for a minute?"

"Right up my alley," Raj responded. "You know how I love anything to do with the brain. I still miss our group coaching sessions where I could talk about neuroscience to my heart's content."

The two reminisced briefly before Kim went on. "This VUCA stuff we've been talking about, Raj. It's helpful to have a label for what's happening and the rate of change, but that's not helping me to deal with it. I feel like I'm in quicksand, constantly shifting. At this rate, it'll soon be over my head." Kim stopped, as the strain in her voice echoed over the phone line.

"I can hear how worried you are, Kim. Let's see if we can stir up a little oxytocin before the cortisol takes over."[11]

"What?" Kim yelped. "What are you talking about, Raj?"

"You asked to pick my brain, Kim, and what has been on my mind is some of the recent research on neurochemicals in our brains. I think it could help us get on the right track today."

Kim sighed, "I should've known. You and your neuroscience obsession. Oh well, what have I got to lose? Let's go for it, Raj. Give me your neuroscience speech."

"My pleasure," Raj agreed. "You remember at the Lunch & Learn session where Patrick focused on Double-Clicking, and mentioned Conversational Intelligence?" At Kim's "Mmm-hmmm," Raj continued. "The essence of Conversational Intelligence is based in research. Now that neuroscientists have the technology to see what is going on in our brains, we know a lot more about trust, connection, and feeling good in relationships. It turns out that when we feel distressed, especially when we distrust another person, we go into 'protect' mode. The neurochemical cortisol is released, which incites a part of our brain called the amygdala. So far so good?"

"I think so, Raj. I remember some of the fight-flight-freeze stuff from school."

"That's it," Raj continued. "That survival part of our brain has helped us to endure throughout our evolution. However, cortisol can work against us when it comes to thriving. It's not designed to help us connect and collaborate. That's where oxytocin comes in. Oxytocin is the 'feel good' chemical in the brain. It's associated with trust, and with activity in our neocortex. That's the part of our brain that enables us to connect, listen, consider, and especially to access the executive decision-making and strategic thinking skills that make us uniquely human."[12]

"That's interesting, Raj, and I've been scribbling notes as you talk. I'm still not sure how it applies to me. I mean, how does that help when I'm feeling uncertain and overwhelmed?" Kim persisted. "It's not just about work; it's home too. The kids are teens now, and they don't need me the way they used to."

Raj smiled, and even though Kim couldn't see him, she could hear the warmth in his voice over the telephone line. "I'm getting to how you can put this into action, Kim. One of the best ways I know to create oxytocin is to build trust. Sometimes it's building trust with others; other times it's with yourself. Reconnecting with your core values is one way to do that. Have you done any thinking about what's most important to you at this point in your life? What do you prioritize when you are faced with a decision?"

"Actually, I have been thinking about what's important to me," Kim admitted. "My daughter Adrienne came home from middle school recently with a values clarification exercise where she had to identify her top five values. I got intrigued and found myself doing it along with her. Excellence. Family. Contribution. Connection. Kindness. That's what I came up with."

"I think you have your answer, Kim. Hearing your confidence when you share those values—I think you have the key to not sinking in the ever-shifting quicksand. Just reconnect to your values, and consider how you can honor them in whatever decision you make. You'll create a sense of balance for yourself. That will enable you to access all your brain power in thinking it through." Raj was excited for his colleague.

"Oxytocin and all?" Kim asked.

"Oxytocin and all!" Raj agreed.

Laughing, the two ended their call.

21

DONNA'S "MAKE IT OR BREAK IT" MOMENT

Patrick greeted Donna as she took a seat in Tech Environments' team lounge. "What's wrong, Donna? You look like you've got bad news."

"Unfortunately, I do. Ted just showed me a report indicating that our revenues are down 4% year over year. We projected a 3% increase, so we are way off on our business development. I really don't know how to share this with the sales team, Patrick. They are going to blame Marketing, or Product Development. Or they'll say that Lynn is tying our hands with all her risk management and compliance demands. But the truth is that it's everything, and everyone. We just can't keep up. We are playing whack-a-mole with all the challenges here at Tech Environments. And it's the same with our customers. The complexity is killing us."

"What are you talking about, Donna? I'm not sure I understand." Patrick looked puzzled, but leaned forward, his posture reflecting that he really wanted to know what she meant.

"If we can't find a way to develop better answers, Patrick, we aren't going to be successful in dealing with this level of complexity. Regardless of whether Jack becomes less controlling, or Lynn and I stop fighting, or

Arun pays attention to how he impacts others." Donna shook her head in despair. "I'm afraid we are going down the tubes, Patrick."

"Hold on there, Donna. Wait a minute. Were you not the one who said we needed to look at our vision and stop focusing on all the threats? As I recall, you guided us in choosing six key indicators to prioritize as we set our strategic direction. What happened to that optimistic, forward-thinking leader?" Patrick gazed at their Marketing VP with concern.

Donna frowned at the recollection. "Maybe you're right. I'm just now recognizing how many challenges we are facing. I feel like I've let the company down, not generating enough new leads to keep us growing. But honestly, there is so much to focus on that it's hard to know where to begin."

"I think you and I are built a lot alike in that way, Donna. We're accustomed to relying on ourselves, solving problems and moving on. One of the hardest things at this point in our growth as a team is figuring out how to rely on one another. Otherwise we'll all be burned out, and Tech Environments won't be viable for the long term. That's why we've hired Edgar to help us with the situation. Did you forget that?"

"I haven't forgotten, Patrick. Guess the pressure is just getting to me. Thanks for trying to talk me off the ledge."

"I'm glad you gave me the opportunity to do that, Donna. We can't rely on our speed and dexterity playing whack-a-mole any longer, as entertaining and engaging as that's been. We've been successful doing it, but I'm afraid it doesn't work anymore. It might be because of VUCA or because we've grown in size, but I think we all recognize that we have to change. Now we just need to find the right blend of planning and execution to take us there. I'm hoping that Edgar will get us started in the right direction."

"I just wish it didn't feel like we have to change overnight," Donna commented, still unsure of the team's ability.

Patrick got up and walked with Donna as she headed out the door. "Hang in there?"

"Will do." Donna agreed.

22

CAN WE DOUBLE-CLICK ON VUCA?

The frequency with which "Double-Clicking" showed up in conversations at Tech Environments in the weeks after Patrick's Lunch & Learn session was amusing, and sometimes annoying. Colleagues often found themselves in discussions where others would prompt them to explain themselves with "Can you Double-Click on that?" Overnight, the new terminology seemed to have become part of their culture.

Even Arun found Double-Clicking useful, as it did not seem to require him to admit when he did not know something. He could simply Double-Click and find out more.

On yet another busy morning, Arun headed in to the TE kitchen and put a green tea k-cup into the coffeemaker. *This VUCA thing*, he thought with irritation. *Everyone else on the SLT has glommed onto VUCA as our new call to action, but it doesn't really make sense to me.* As his tea was dispensed by the machine, Lynn came in, greeted Arun, and selected a French Roast coffee pod, waiting for the Keurig to be freed up for her third cup of the day.

"Lynn, do you have a minute while your coffee's brewing?" Arun asked.

Glancing at her watch, Lynn reported, "I have exactly 24 minutes before my next meeting, Arun. What do you need?"

On unfamiliar ground, Arun paused, but plunged ahead. "I get the gist of VUCA, Lynn. I know what those four letters stand for. However, it's not apparent to me what it really means or how it helps us. Could you Double-Click on VUCA for me when it comes to us moving forward as a company?"

"Glad to, Arun. Let me just grab my coffee and we can sit down for a few minutes."

At the counter, Lynn quickly retrieved her iPad to show Arun a table she'd created :

Issue	Action
Volatility	Realize you can count on volatility. Regardless of your priorities, things change quickly. Identify what you can rely on: organizational and core values, processes, what's not changing. Discover or create havens of stability, and create bandwidth and procedures for more agile responses.
Uncertainty	Don't assume that what you've always done will still work. Take a fresh look at situations and challenge your assumptions. Partner with others. Recognize that uncertainty is a characteristic of the learning process.
Complexity	Teamwork. Deal with the volume of information by ensuring you see the whole picture and by leveraging your entire team. Develop systems for organizing the data you have. Ask curious questions. Invest in growing your team. Avoid silos.
Ambiguity	Recognize the inefficiencies that occur when things are unclear, and provide clear direction. Listen for underlying meanings and priorities. Double-Click often. Celebrate accomplishments along the way.

When Arun had finished reviewing what Lynn had shared, he nodded his head. "It doesn't fill in all the gaps, Lynn, but it does make VUCA seem like a call to action and not just a catchy acronym. Do you mind sending this to me? In fact, I wonder if it would be useful for everyone on the SLT? If I have questions, then we all do. And it appears that several of your action steps involve developing teamwork and mutual understanding."

"Good idea, Arun. I created this for my own clarity, and it doesn't make sense to keep it to myself. Now that we're talking, I'm aware that you and others will add to it and make it better. I'll send it now."

As Arun finished his tea and rinsed out his mug, he found himself whistling. *I still have to meet with Jordan,* he reminded himself, *and work on the whole bullying thing. But maybe I am beginning to be a little clearer about how to move forward.*

PART 2

MOVING FORWARD

23

LYNN AND DONNA SEE SOMETHING NEW

"Thanks for being willing to come to my office," Donna gestured to Lynn to make herself comfortable in the stylish seating area.

After pouring them both a glass of water, Donna opened the conversation. "What did you think of the TED* book I suggested that both of us read? And, more to the point, what have you been thinking about trying to improve our relationship?"

Lynn sat down and paused before responding. "I was irritated at first, to be honest with you. I didn't think it was a big issue. On the other hand, I respect you, so I stepped back to take an honest look at myself. I see your point. Sometimes the rest of the team tiptoes around the two of us, like they are reluctant to get too close to a hornet's nest. As much as I wanted to believe you were wrong about this, I don't think you are." Lynn raised her eyes to see how Donna might react.

"I read the book," Lynn continued. "I don't like business fables as a rule, and I didn't expect to like this one. In fact, I went straight to the end to see if there was some kind of a cheat sheet there, and I found a summary of the model."

"Huh. I usually skip the end matter of a book," Donna admitted. "What did it say?"

Lynn smiled ruefully. "It basically described the dance that we do all the time. You know—I experience you as a pain and see myself as innocent. You view me as irritating, and yourself as darn close to perfect. We've got two of the three roles nailed—Persecutor and Victim—in what the model calls the Dreaded Drama Triangle. The third role is the Rescuer, which I guess is the role the others have been playing when they try to calm us down or distract us. Pretty accurate depiction, I had to admit." Lynn took a long swallow of her water.

Looking at one another, the two women began to laugh. Donna got hold of herself first and spoke. "After I got over feeling dismayed at realizing how much energy we've put into our minor feud, I have to confess that the story captured my attention. It described us pretty accurately. I also recognize that we aren't the only ones doing the drama dance, which is a relief."

"So you just read the fable part and got the same interpretation I did?" Lynn asked.

Donna nodded. "Yes, I enjoy a good story. This one got my attention. It was easy to see how we make ourselves, and each other, miserable. As I read, I began to feel hopeful there might be a different way to deal with things, without sacrificing our own unique styles. I ended up appreciating the possibility of changing the way we interact. The alternative to drama, focusing on the desired outcome, is a natural way for me to think in most situations. When it comes to you, I realize that I've concentrated on the negative. I've seen you as an obstacle and a problem. I respect your expertise when it comes to risk management, but I get impatient and annoyed when you want to verify everything. I just didn't realize my irritation was so obvious to you, and to everyone else."

"Same here," agreed Lynn. "Once I recognized myself in the drama triangle, I was eager for a resolution. Especially when I realized that we are destined to keep repeating the same pattern until we make a conscious shift. It made sense to me that focusing on the outcome would help us to work together, to see our differences as equally valid paths to a shared goal. It seems so simple now that I see it. So, what's next?" she asked.

"That's what I wanted to ask you," Donna replied. "I appreciate a good story, and this is certainly one we could share with others if we are willing. Would you be up for doing that? I have the sense that others would recognize themselves in our experiences."

"Who would we tell the story to?" Lynn wondered.

Donna was excited now. "I have just the group, and there's an opportunity coming up." Seeing Lynn's curious expression, she continued, "Have you heard about the STEM Women Leaders Forum that Kim and Jen and some others created for the next generation of women tech leaders in our community? The forum is meeting next month here at Tech Environments, and Kim is responsible for creating the program. Ever heard of the group?"

Lynn shook her head, "No, but I have a feeling I'm going to."

24

DRAMA: A CAUTIONARY TALE FOR WOMEN IN TECHNOLOGY

"Testing 1, 2, 3. Testing 1, 2, 3. Looks like we are all set." Kim stepped up to the podium and spoke into the microphone to quiet the room full of 70 or so women attending the STEM Women Leaders Forum. "Welcome. We're happy to host you at Tech Environments this month. As you know, I'm a senior team lead here, and part of our internal coaching initiative," Kim announced. "We feel like we are on the leading edge here in supporting a diverse workforce." Everyone applauded.

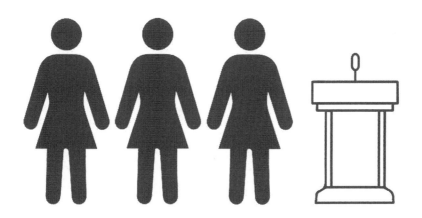

Kim continued, "I'd like to introduce to you two women who many of you already know—Lynn Atom, our Chief Risk Officer at Tech Environments, and Donna Stillworth, our Chief Marketing Officer. Lynn and Donna have both been featured in numerous articles on C-suite women leaders who are creating a more diverse workforce in our industry. They have generously agreed to be with us today to tell their stories and the lessons they learned along the way. I believe that Lynn and Donna sharing their wisdom will save all of us time, energy, and missteps on our own career journeys. I'm excited to hear what they have to say, and I am sure you'll appreciate it as well." The audience applauded as Donna and Lynn joined Kim on the stage, seating themselves comfortably on a trio of chairs.

Donna took the mic first. "I'd like to tell you about the worst leader I've ever had to work with." She glanced out at the audience, who already appeared riveted. "The leader I'm talking about was opinionated, irritatingly deliberate, and always, always, ALWAYS believed she was right. In an industry like ours that thrives on innovation, this leader's aversion to risk was legendary. She handcuffed us—we could never try anything new without her presenting roadblock after roadblock to our work. Obviously, she was an obstacle to progress, a hindrance to the entire team. I was convinced that if someone did not challenge her, our company would be extinct in no time at all. I made it my business to do everything I could to keep her from getting her way." Donna looked out at the audience and observed many heads nodding in agreement. She spoke into the microphone once more, "And I'm not the only one who has had to deal with a problem leader. Lynn has had a similar experience."

Accepting the microphone with a nod, Lynn declared, "As terrible of a leader as the one Donna described sounds, you'll have to agree that the leader I'm going to tell you about was ten times worse. This leader was impulsive, thoughtless, and reckless. She—yes, it was a woman again—was a loose cannon. Whenever I was on a project with this leader, I'd spend the entire time biting my nails, never sure when she would suggest some half-baked idea that would cost the company money and valuable time, not to mention our reputation. To tell you the truth, I had no idea how this person ever got promoted to the position she held in the organization. She scared the bejeezus out of me. I knew I had to rein her in. There was no doubt in my mind she was going to bankrupt us, or worse." Appreciating the tense expressions on the faces of their audience as everyone listened to her description, Lynn returned the mic to Kim as MC.

Kim now addressed her colleagues on the stage with the question on everyone's minds: "Two horrendous leaders, and each of you responsible for preventing them from doing damage to the company! What did you do?"

Lynn took the mic first, "As you can imagine, I did everything in my power to prevent this woman from destroying what we had built. I told everyone who would listen about her. I put policies in place to limit her budgetary authority. I vetoed her inclusion in key decisions. I just knew I had to protect us." Lynn passed the microphone to Donna.

Donna nodded her agreement. "Like Lynn, I was determined that this leader should not ruin what we had created. I strived to ensure that she wouldn't get in the way of our further achievements. I found ways to go around her as often as possible. I made sure I had the ear of the CEO and the CFO. I admit I spent quite a few sleepless nights planning for how we might get rid of her." Donna frowned at the memory.

Kim shook her head in dismay as she retrieved the microphone. "It's hard to believe that both of you had to deal with such inept, ineffective leaders. Thank goodness you found ways around them to accomplish all that you have. Otherwise we would not be listening to you both here today. I know that all of us would like to avoid the two leaders you describe as we move ahead in our own careers. Would you be willing to share who they were so none of us fall into the same trap you both were in?" Kim looked back and forth at Lynn and Donna, eager for their response. At their nods, Kim asked, "Who were they?"

Simultaneously, Donna and Lynn stood up, raised their right arms, and pointed directly at one another. The room erupted in sounds of surprise, laughter, and disbelief. Kim gave the audience a minute before she could quiet them. "Wow! Lynn and Donna, you've certainly shocked us. I experience you both as such wonderful leaders. What happened?"

Now Lynn and Donna stood up together and smiled out at the audience. Lynn spoke first, "So long as I focused on Donna as the villain, I treated her like the problem I believed her to be. As I just told you, I excluded Donna from key meetings and decisions. I tried to sabotage her by limiting her budgetary authority. I was Donna's worst nightmare."

"And I was the same way with Lynn," admitted Donna. "Because I insisted on seeing her as intent on doing damage to the company, I was hell-bent on preventing her from succeeding. You would never have guessed we were on the same team, not from the way I acted."

A woman in the audience blurted out, "But you seem like you respect each other so much. And you've won all these awards. What changed?" The speaker seemed desperate to know.

"We shifted our focus," Donna said. "It sounds simple, but it was extremely challenging at first. We had to make a conscious choice to stop seeing each other as problems. Instead, we got clear about what we wanted. We chose an outcome important to both of us, and we committed to working together toward that end. From the moment of that decision, whenever our approaches differed, we stayed true to our commitment to respect the other's input and to learn from her perspective."

"And it was the strangest thing," Lynn took over. "Donna became one of my most trusted colleagues, the leader I count on most to show me my blind spots and challenge me to become better. Once we realized that we both wanted the company to flourish, we translated that desire into helping one another succeed. In the process, we've both grown. Sharing our story with you is one way to honor a shared vision we hold of having more women leaders in senior roles in technology. And it never hurts to remind ourselves to value our unique approaches, to see our differences as a challenge and an opportunity instead of as a problem."

The audience broke out in spontaneous applause as Kim stood up and shook Lynn's and Donna's hands. "Thank you so much for a powerful account of your journeys, and a cautionary tale for all of us. When we are convinced that we are right, it's natural to view those who disagree as barriers and problems. You've shown us an alternative that seems much more powerful."

Turning back to the audience, Kim brought the meeting to a conclusion, "Thank you all for being here today. You may have noticed that in the goody bags you've received there's a book called *The Power of TED**, and a personal link to an online program called *3 Vital Questions*[13]. These are resources Donna and Lynn used as they made the shift that they talked about today. The book and course are our gift to you as members of this group. We'd love to hear your own stories as you apply what you learn to the drama in your lives." Applause broke out once more as participants got up and gathered their belongings. Animated conversations continued as Lynn, Donna, and Kim high-fived one another, enjoying the moment.

25

WELL? HOW ARE WE DOING?

Edgar felt hopeful as he anticipated the meeting he'd scheduled with the team. *I have much more data on Tech Environments' challenges than when I first got back here a month ago. I wonder if others have been consciously noticing and reflecting too, not just on VUCA but on sustainability in general. Their input is crucial.*

Halfway through his two months of providing his sustainability services for free, Edgar had requested a check-in meeting to assess progress. He wanted to have a holistic and honest conversation about where they stood. To that end, Edgar had sent the agenda in advance, posing three questions:

1. What problems have we identified so far when it comes to Tech Environments' success?
2. What progress have we made in addressing them?
3. What other barriers exist to sustainable success? (Consider financial, people, products, processes, habits, mindsets, competencies, reputation, and anything else that comes to mind.)

It's only three questions, Edgar thought, *but anyone who'd committed to really try to answer them would have to devote a fair amount of thought and effort. I hope they found the time to do that.*

The senior leadership team seemed energized as they arrived for the session. With the SLT members' support, Edgar had invited several other company leaders to attend and offer their input. *Sometimes the SLT gets too insular and doesn't even recognize what they are not seeing. Having other perspectives will help with that,* he reasoned, *plus I've noticed that they typically behave better with one another when others are present. We'll accomplish more.*

In response to Edgar's invitation, middle managers Kim, Raj, Marianne, Javy, and Jen filed into the room right behind Ted and Donna. These high-potential leaders appeared excited but slightly subdued at the moment. Three had been part of the group coaching initiative at Tech Environments several years earlier, so having a candid conversation with curious questions was not a foreign concept. Still, Javy and Jen in particular seemed a little tentative as they took their seats. *Pretty normal for them to be at least a little anxious,* Edgar thought. *They are all aware that this is an opportunity for them to gain visibility and credibility with the senior leaders. Here's hoping I can get them comfortable. We need a good level of trust if we are going to make headway.*

Edgar began the meeting by reminding everyone that the SLT had identified six key indicators that they deemed necessary for Tech Environments' sustainability from their vantage point. These were displayed on the smart board:

1. Values: A set of clear and relevant values that give us a road map to work and live by
2. Engagement: An engaged team of associates who see themselves as problem solvers and want to be here
3. Innovation: An updated and expanded set of products and methodologies to offer our clients
4. Leadership: Leaders who are role models for the values we espouse
5. Revenues: Robust revenues that enable confidence and growth

6. Reputation: Positive visibility in the press regarding our culture and our positive impact for our clients and community

Edgar inquired, "So if you had all six of these, you'd be confident that Tech Environments had everything it needs, everything you require, to be sustainable for the long term?" The six senior leaders, already familiar with the indicators, quickly nodded their heads. The session's additional attendees studied the list. After giving them a few minutes, Edgar checked in, "What do you think? If the company aced each of these, would we be successful well into the future?"

"I believe so," voiced Kim, as she looked at her own notes. "Everything that I came up with in response to your questions about problems and progress aligns with one or more of those." Perceiving that other heads were nodding in agreement, Edgar distributed three flip chart easels so there was one by each of the three tables.

"Here's the structure we'll use for the meeting today," he announced. "I sent you three questions to prepare for our dialogue, and I'd like you each to have the opportunity to share your responses to all three. That will be easier in small groups. Each group will circulate around to each of the flip charts, documenting your wisdom in response to the three questions, one on each flip chart. Clear?" Seeing their agreement, Edgar anticipated one likely event. "When you move to your second-round question, read what's already written there and put an asterisk next to anything already listed that you want to echo. Add any new items. Then during the third round, finalize the list with additional points, and star the repeats. Whichever easel you end with, you'll be reporting out on the whole list for that question. We'll spend fifteen minutes for the first round, and then ten for each subsequent round. Go for it!"

The leaders scattered around the room to their designated easels. Jen scribed for the first group, listening to Donna's and Ted's responses to the question about problems identified, while also interspersing her own.

Patrick recorded the second group's input, looking surprised at how much progress the group felt that they'd already made. Capturing the third group's identification of barriers to sustainability, Raj struggled to keep up with the group's input on all the potential challenges. At the end of the exercise, the small groups had rotated to all three easels. Edgar recognized that they seemed to be done, and called time. "Each group now needs to share what you have on your flip chart with the whole group."

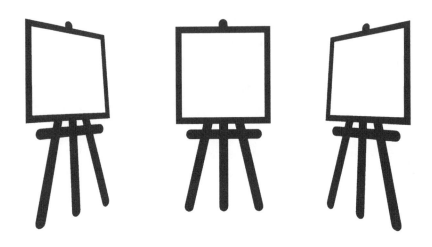

Raj highlighted question 1 responses to the problems that had been identified for Tech Environments—lower revenues, morale, technology changes, shrinking client budgets, and a category that he just labeled "VUCA." Edgar thanked him, and, not wanting to dwell on problems, prompted, "Okay, before we get depressed by the prospect of all the problems, let's hear answers to question 2 on progress to date."

Jack stepped up now. "Morale and teamwork are improving. We've seen the peer coaching continue to reap dividends for the senior team, and Kim and others see the same thing in the next tier of leaders. So that's a win. Other progress includes our recent discovery of equine coaching, which has helped your CEO recognize that he cannot control, or do, everything by himself." Everyone laughed, with Arun feigning a look of shock. Jack continued, "And then we have seen many team members Double-Clicking for clarity where they used to just make assumptions. Our reputation seems to be turning around too: as all of you know, Donna and Lynn impressed the Women's Leadership Forum last week with their leadership stories. We've also gotten some positive press in our clients' publications." Jack quickly glanced at the list to be sure he'd covered everything before concluding. "It's good to see some progress."

"Excellent list! Question 3?" Edgar requested. Jen got up and stated, "As you can see, we've still got work left to do. We have to use the resources and sustain the progress that Jack just talked about. We believe that the biggest challenges still facing us are 1 and 2 on the list of key metrics— getting clear about our commitment to shared values, and fully engaging our team. Integrity in putting our values into action, and consistently involving all associates in sharing ideas and creating strategies. Those are the things that provide the foundation for innovation, revenues, and positive reputation. Transparency is still a challenge, and one reason that Donna and Lynn's presentation was so powerful. We need our most senior leaders to be role models for our values of Integrity, Innovation, and Impact." Jen sat down, looking slightly nervous but also pleased.

Edgar recognized afterwards that he needn't have spent the effort worrying about the middle managers being too anxious to contribute. *They are on fire,* he thought. *It was the right choice to include them as part of our succession plan, and good to have fresh eyes open around the company to gather data as we go forward. All in all,* Edgar smiled, *a successful meeting.*

26

IS THE CHIEF PEOPLE OFFICER A FRAUD?

Jordan's office was a brisk 20-minute walk from the Tech Environments' campus, and Patrick was slightly out of breath when he arrived. *I thought if I walked here I'd feel a little more centered*, he reflected, *but if anything I feel even more anxious after obsessing the whole way here. Our meeting on progress and problems shows we still have a long way to go. And I wonder how much of it is my fault that we are experiencing so many challenges.*

"What's on your mind, Patrick?" Jordan greeted him. "It's not often you request an emergency coaching session."

Patrick launched in, "While my old boss Ellen was still at Tech Environments as Chief People Officer, I always had a safety net. Even though I wanted to keep moving up in the organization, I genuinely liked being Ellen's second in command. It was easy to take risks and try things. I trusted she would bail me out if something went wrong. Ellen gave me a lot of autonomy, for sure, but she was always there. Now I feel like an impostor, a fraud. Most of the issues facing us could have been prevented if I had handled some of the people issues—Jack's self-reliance, Arun's bruising style, the stressful relationship Donna and Lynn have experienced. Ellen wouldn't have let this happen. I blame myself for not handling this more proactively."

"I'm surprised to hear that, Patrick. You have accomplished so much since Ellen left that it's curious to me that you are so focused on the problems. What is it you expect of yourself?" Jordan encouraged him.

Patrick was ready with his answer. "I've thought about that a lot. As Chief People Officer I am supposed to ensure a positive culture where people thrive. It's up to me to resolve personnel issues—to handle them promptly and effectively so everyone can get back to doing their jobs. I should be one step ahead of others in noticing people issues before they have a negative impact. And it's my responsibility to motivate staff and to prevent conflicts that might escalate. Of course, any harassment issues are my job to handle, and . . ." Patrick's voice trailed off as he realized that Jordan was regarding him with an amused expression. "What?" he asked. "Did I say something funny?"

"If I'm not mistaken, you just described Superman," Jordan responded. "You were just getting to the part about how you ought to be able to read people's minds with your x-ray vision."

"No, really! There's so much I should be doing, so much at stake," Patrick asserted. "It seems like you of all people would see that. I'm just realizing I probably wasn't ready to take this on. If Ellen had stayed longer, I would've had the chance to learn more from her."

"I can see you are stressed, Patrick, and I can certainly tell that it's important to you to do a good job. What I'm less sure about is that it's up to you alone," Jordan observed.

Patrick looked startled. "What do you mean?"

"It's a big title, Patrick—'Chief People Officer.' You are right about that. But I don't think it is meant to suggest you're expected do all those things solo. You have a good team there supporting you. Maybe it's more of an 'us' than just you?" Jordan's voice was gentle now.

"When you say that, it seems kind of absurd. I hadn't really thought of it that way." Patrick was quiet for a minute. "Even if it's not all up to me, I guess I'm still not sure what to do about how I'm feeling," he finally continued. "I keep wondering if I'm cut out for this role."

"How would you know?" Jordan inquired.

Patrick shrugged, so Jordan probed, "What are the bright spots—the times you feel effective?"

Patrick stared out the window for a moment before offering a response. "I guess I felt pretty good about the Lunch & Learn I did a while back. The response was good, and I've heard people using the term 'Double-Click' since then when there's some disagreement and they aren't on the same page. 'Double-Click' seems to have gotten added to our language for exploring differences."

Jordan nodded. "That's good. I remember Donna talking about using that in business development as well to clarify what your customers want. What else?"

Patrick shook his head, but then remembered something. "Well, Jack and I had a candid conversation with Arun recently. It wasn't easy, but I felt good about the way I supported Jack in getting clear about what he needed to say, and giving Arun the space to decide what he is going to do about the problem."

"Both great examples, Patrick. What else?"

"I can't think of anything else right now, Jordan, but it's helpful to realize that I'm doing at least a few things right." Patrick offered with a smile. "It was great of you to fit me in today. I've appreciated how you support others on our team, but I somehow overlooked the fact that I could use a little coaching myself. Thank you." He shook Jordan's hand and headed out the door.

Patrick was surprised at how much calmer he felt on the walk back to Tech Environments. *I've been so afraid of making a mistake that I haven't been noticing the good stuff. Whether I leave Tech Environments to go work with Ellen again or not, I guess it wouldn't hurt to start relying on others a little more. Maybe I'd feel a little better if I didn't assume it's all on me.*

27

WHAT SHOULD WE DO ABOUT THE RISKS?

For Lynn and Patrick, agreeing on a time to address a shared concern had been easy. Figuring out how to address the matter was anything but. Lynn was pensive as she headed for her meeting with Patrick. *Workplace harassment is yet another example of VUCA,* she thought. *Volatile without a doubt. Uncertain, though I am positive it's going to get worse if we don't address it. Complex for sure—there are a lot of stakeholders and a great deal at stake. And definitely Ambiguous—it's not clear what the core issue is because attitude and perception are hard things to nail down. Another experience of VUCA for sure, this one involving our internal climate and culture instead of external factors. I hope Patrick's got something up his sleeve.*

Lynn had by now arrived at Patrick's office, and found his door open. Forgoing preliminary chitchat, she greeted her colleague, "Hi, Patrick. I hope you had a chance to read the bullet points I sent you about harassment reports and risks."

"I did, Lynn. Sounds as if the perception of Arun as a bully has taken on a life of its own. It concerns me. He is such a solid person underneath his brusque exterior. I'd like to see him able to turn it around." Opening his laptop and pulling up the Glassdoor.com site, Patrick reminded Lynn of his own worries in addition to what she had shared. He pointed at the screen, "And there are the online posts. I know you are aware that we've gotten several negative reviews on this job seekers' website. Two of the posts speak to gender bias and harassment here." Patrick turned the screen to Lynn so she could refamiliarize herself with the comments.

When she'd finished reading, Lynn nodded. "Clearly, we've got some work to do, Patrick. I've got my own opinions about this. What are you thinking?" She queried her colleague.

"You know, Lynn, I've been doing a lot of soul searching. We did not address Arun's behavior soon enough. All of us on the SLT know him well, and we trusted there was no malice in his behavior. However, he was oblivious to its impact on less senior team members. And we overlooked the importance of Arun as a role model for appropriate behavior." Patrick shook his head, experiencing again the disappointment he'd felt on comprehending just how negative Arun's impact had been. "You are aware that Jack and I met with Arun to speak to the issue. Arun is very clear now that he has a problem. I know he plans to address it, and I hope he'll be successful. What else do we need to do meanwhile to respond to the other concerns?"

"I'm worried about Arun, of course," Lynn answered. "But the Glassdoor posts suggest we have a bigger issue. I have an idea, but it's really outside of my expertise," Lynn said tentatively.

Patrick was curious. "I'm all ears, Lynn. What are you thinking?"

"As you know, my preference is to minimize risks. I'd rather prevent negative situations that we'll have to handle. I develop policies and plans, and purchase the necessary insurance. We have those things in place when it comes to harassment. However, I don't think we've ever had an active anti-bullying or harassment reaction program. I have heard from some colleagues that they can be quite effective." Lynn paused to gauge Patrick's reaction.

"Hmmmmm. I guess you're right, Lynn. We have the online orientation modules that new hires all go through when it comes to harassment, but we haven't done much more than that. It hadn't appeared to be a significant issue up until now," Patrick responded.

"I don't think a passive informational approach is enough anymore," continued Lynn with more confidence. "I'd like us to create something that puts everyone in a position of power. Each person—bully, bullied, witness, boss—should know what action to take when it comes to bullying or harassment."

Patrick smiled. "I like where you are headed, Lynn. I especially like the idea of us all owning responsibility for the climate we create here. We could form a cross-department project team to shape the program. Do you think those who have been harassed or bullied would be willing to be part of developing a solution?"

Lynn nodded. "I think so, Patrick. The people who've made formal complaints have all been supported by their managers in bringing issues to my attention. There are probably others, like those who've posted on Glassdoor, who haven't felt safe enough to be upfront. But at least we can identify a few people. I expect they would be delighted to see we are doing something about this." Lynn was confident in her assessment.

"That's good to know," Patrick responded. "My colleague Marianne has been looking for an opportunity to direct an initiative. I'd like her to take the lead. Any concern about that?"

"That makes sense to me," Lynn concurred. "Let's see what she comes up with. I'm excited about this, Patrick. I think we are turning a bad situation into something that could be a real opportunity for us to be better." Lynn reached out to high-five her colleague as she gathered her materials to leave. "Nice job. You've put me at ease."

That was good, reflected Patrick as Lynn left his office. *I guess Jordan was right—I've been so focused on worrying that I don't know what I'm doing that I haven't noticed that I have grown into filling this role just fine. Feels pretty good at the moment.* Patrick smiled to himself. Then he headed out the door to tell Marianne the good news about her opportunity for a stretch assignment.

28

APPARENTLY ARUN MUST CHANGE, BUT HOW?

Arun's thoughts were swirling. *Is this bullying thing that big a deal? I really need to be building our product pipeline and not be worrying about people's feelings. But Patrick seemed so serious, and I'm not sure I can do nothing.* Shaking his head to clear it, he entered Jordan's office building.

Minutes later, Arun settled into the chair in Jordan's office. He did not hesitate to start the coaching session with why he was there. "No offense, Jordan, but I only scheduled this session because Jack and Patrick insisted on it. They have an issue with how I am acting toward others. And if they have a problem with me, then I have a problem."

"Okay, Arun, so what is it that you want from our coaching today?" Jordan responded, curious about whether Arun was simply complying with an edict or would choose to make good use of their time.

"You know how I am, Jordan. I can be abrupt with people, but I never intend to hurt their feelings. I work hard. I am ambitious. I am confident. I just expect others to understand it's not personal. We have a job to get done." Arun sat back in his chair, having spoken his piece.

"What else?" Jordan pushed.

"With products, I am always eager for feedback. I don't mind when new initiatives fail early in the process. In fact, with the agile process we employ, frequent failures are a given. We get feedback, improve the product, and try again. I keep trying to see how that process could work for me. How can I improve? It's unclear to me what to do with the feedback when others feel hurt by my behavior. Injuring others is never my intent."

"What happens if nothing changes?" Jordan prompted.

Arun grimaced. "That's just it. Jack pretty much gave me an ultimatum that something has to change. Having Patrick sit in on the meeting in his official role as Chief People Officer lets me know it's serious. Apparently they have received a number of complaints over the years but now at least one person has initiated our formal grievance procedure. I'd like to say that the person complaining should have talked to me first, but apparently they tried. I don't tend to pay much attention to complaints."

"So, if nothing changes?" Jordan repeated.

"If nothing changes, it's hard to imagine that they would actually terminate me. I am a well-respected technology leader, and very skilled in my role. However, I recognize that integrity is becoming increasingly central to the way we operate. I look at the three values we recently identified with Edgar's help—Integrity, Innovation, and Impact. The only one I feel truly aligned with is Innovation. Apparently, I am having a negative impact on others at the company, and am out of integrity with our three espoused values. I do not believe that is acceptable or sustainable." Arun cleared his throat, but didn't continue.

"You have a gap," Jordan observed. "A gap between the present state, where your direct style is having a negative impact, and your desired future state, where your style is effective and yet still authentic to you. Do I have that right?"

"Yes, that's it exactly!" Arun exclaimed, pleased to have it articulated so clearly. "But how do I close the gap?"

116

Jordan considered his request, but instead of answering, responded with another question. "When have you been effective in managing your tone with others, Arun? When have you received feedback that others have enjoyed being with you, and not just accomplishing a task together?"

"Not often at work," Arun acknowledged. "Many people have known me long enough that they cut me a great deal of slack. They don't take my bluntness personally, but I would not say they enjoy it. Patrick and I have continued as peer coaching buddies for the past two years, and we have developed effective ways to give honest feedback to one another. Patrick is one of the few who have called me on my behavior, and that's probably because he is a peer and not a direct report. Others are willing to work with me mainly because we have the opportunity to develop innovative products and processes. We do good work together."

"You said it doesn't happen often at work that you get positive feedback that's unrelated to the task itself. Does it ever happen outside of work?" Jordan inquired. She was surprised to see Arun's expression soften.

Arun smiled for the first time. "As you know, I have a family—a wife and two boys. They sometimes accuse me of being a bear, but I find that it is easy to hear that from them. My job at home is to be a good husband and father. Their feedback helps me do those things better. I try, and sometimes they tell me I succeed," Arun chuckled.

Jordan joined Arun in laughing before asking another question. "What seems to enable you to change your tone successfully at home, Arun? As you put it, what helps you not to be such a bear?"

This time, the look on Arun's face was one of pride. "My boys are incredible. They are active, curious, smart, and challenging. I was that way when I was young too, but my own father did not appreciate being challenged. I am a different kind of father. With my boys, I encourage their thought-provoking questions, and I thoroughly enjoy them."

"I can tell you are proud of them, and committed to being a good father. And with your wife? What helps you there?" Jordan persisted.

"My wife is also honest with me, and does not accept a tone she considers harsh or condescending. We have worked on that over the years and I have improved. Training for the half marathon this year has had an unexpected benefit, in that running seems to help me stay more calm and centered. Nowadays, if I am too sharp with my wife or the boys, my wife tells me to go for a run. It has become code for asking me to self-correct my behavior. Usually I take her advice and am in a better space when I return." Arun nodded his head twice, as if confirming something for himself.

Seeing this, Jordan asked, "It looks like you just had something click for you, Arun. What is it?"

"Yes, something did click. Two things, as a matter of fact. Raj has been talking with me, with many of us at Tech Environments, about neuroscience. Raj highlights what we can do to down-regulate the cortisol we produce under stress, and to up-regulate oxytocin, the neurotransmitter associated with relationships and bonding.[14] It occurred to me that I have more oxytocin-inducing conversations at home than I do at work. As a result, my family gets a better version of me," Arun declared.

"Powerful awareness, Arun," Jordan affirmed. "What next step can you take now that you see that?"

Now Arun shifted uncomfortably in his seat. "Unfortunately, the next steps will be difficult ones for me. I will have to be transparent, and I will need to apologize. Transparent with my team about the fact that I am working on my tendency to be abrupt, even rude. I will ask them for feedback about when my manner is more positive and when I am causing them stress."

"Is that the difficult part for you?" inquired Jordan.

"Yes, that will be difficult, but the apology is even harder. Because I do not intend to injure others, I do not believe I owe anyone an apology. However, I *am* hurting others, and I can see now that it is hurting the company too. If people are complaining about me, they are unable to focus effectively on their work. And, again, Raj tells me that, according to neuroscience, we are far less creative and innovative when trust is not present. I will need to apologize about my negative impact as a first step to rebuilding trust," he said with determination.

"Anything else?"

"Perhaps it wouldn't be a bad idea to keep a set of running shoes and clothes at work," Arun commented. "Going for a quick run is much better than generating more opportunities for apologies."

"It sounds like you have a strategy, Arun. I am impressed with how much you are putting in to this. You are clearly determined. I know that it won't be easy to execute your plan. I trust that you'll get some valuable feedback as you do so."

"Thank you, Jordan. I needed that." Arun nodded his appreciation as he strode from the office.

29

CREATING A NO BULLY CULTURE

Patrick turned off his computer monitor and checked his phone messages while he waited for Marianne to arrive. She entered his office, a few minutes early as usual.

"How's it going with the bully program planning?" Patrick opened the conversation.

"The Culture Club had our first planning session," Marianne reported. "There are only five of us, so it was easy to find a time that worked in all of our schedules."

"Culture Club? Isn't that a band?" Patrick's obvious confusion caused Marianne to grin.

"Oh. I forgot you didn't know. The anti-bullying team wanted to come up with a positive name for what we are doing. We landed on Culture Club, no relation to the band. We felt like that was what we are about—improving the culture here—and that everyone wants to be part of a club."

"I like it." Patrick complimented the name choice. "How does the group think we should move forward?"

"We've found some good resources." Marianne spread out several documents across the table. "There are quite a few anti-bullying initiatives out there. The ones we like best ensure that each person knows his or her role when a situation arises. For the bully, the action is 'find something to do besides bullying.' For the bully's boss, it's 'hold your bully accountable for being better.' We are creating some good role plays that I think you'll enjoy. You know some of the actors. Can we get twenty minutes on the agenda at the all-hands meeting to introduce the program?"

"That's in only three weeks. Are you sure you'll be ready?" Patrick was astonished at how quickly Marianne was moving the project forward.

"Yes, we'll be ready. Also, you asked me to run it by Lynn so she'd be aware of what we are doing. She's good on it, hopeful that it will help our team's awareness."

"Wow! You jumped in with both feet, Marianne. I'm impressed. Anything you need from me?" Patrick asked.

"Glad you asked, Patrick. There's a nonprofit organization called 'Start with Decency' that focuses on creating civil dialogue. I haven't had a chance to reach out to them yet. Would you be willing to do that? We'd like to know if they are looking for business partners to bring what they are doing to organizations. The web site is www.startwithdecency.org.[15]"

"Sure thing, Marianne. It sounds intriguing. And thanks for throwing me a bone. I was just beginning to think you didn't need me." Patrick shook his head in mock dismay.

Marianne laughed, but answered seriously. "I appreciate your trust in letting me lead this, Patrick. I know it hasn't always been easy for you to delegate and let go. I want you to know how much it means to me."

"You earned it, Marianne, and clearly you're ready. Can't wait to see what this anti-bully culture club comes up with. Here's hoping it helps with our online reputation too."

30

WHO'S RIGHT AND WHO'S WRONG?

Jordan was happy to be with Tech Environments' senior leaders again. Her recent one-on-one sessions with Arun and Patrick had given her a sense of how hard some members of the team were working. It had been awhile since she had worked with the entire SLT, and she was eager to learn more.

Ted surprised everyone by launching right into the session. "As CFO, I've tended to focus mostly on our financials. But lately I've been focusing more on our performance as a whole. Here's something I'm wondering about—we agreed on a set of clear and relevant values that give Tech Environments a road map to navigate by. But how are we going to resolve the individual differences we have in the values we hold? Some of us see things pretty much the opposite of each other. For example, when Arun champions innovation, I bring up tradition."

Arun immediately agreed, "We all have experienced that, and it's usually not a pretty sight."

Ted continued, "It's not just Arun and me differing. Jack advocates individual goals and Patrick says team goals. We are sometimes so opposite in what we believe that shared values can be hard to come by. I just want to minimize our risks of failure."

Lynn added her two cents, "You are clearly right, Ted, when it comes to minimizing risk. We can't afford to make mistakes."

"I don't agree," Donna immediately challenged her colleague. "If we don't take risks and lead the pack with new products, we won't have anything to offer. Our customers are very clear about that. Arun is definitely in the right on that one."

Jack, Patrick, and Coach Jordan all burst out laughing at the vivid example of how hard it was for any two of them to agree on the right approach, let alone all six of them.

Jordan thoughtfully mused, "Then maybe you don't have to agree."

Now it was Jack's turn to differ. "I know you coach with a lot of teams, Jordan, but I can't believe that you encourage them to fight with each other. As CEO, I'll just decide who's right before I'll let us waste our time and energy with infighting."

Everyone now looked to Jordan for her reaction. Patrick shifted in his seat, uncomfortable and uncertain of how to support their coach. By now, however, Jordan was accustomed to Jack's seizing control whenever he felt uncertain. "Jack, why do you have six people on this team to lead the company? Why don't you just head TE solo?"

"Well, of course I often try to do it all by myself, Jordan, as you've noticed," Jack commented ruefully, accompanied by the acknowledging chuckles of his team. "But if you are serious about why it's a team instead of just me, I'd say it's because of the range of opinions we represent. We need that diversity."

"Okay," responded Jordan. "Then let's go back to Ted's question. If you need unique perspectives, and yet some of you can't agree, how will you leverage the diversity instead of choosing sides?"

Lynn spoke up, "Maybe it's just the nature of VUCA? Just an expected result of the uncertainty, complexity, and ambiguity? All teams struggle with collaboration. If that's the case, we might be stuck with it."

"I don't think so," countered Jordan. "I've observed that when you acknowledge the importance of both perspectives, you seem much more capable in dealing with complex challenges. In fact, I am pretty certain that if you stop trying to win when you have a difference in opinion, you'll be even more effective. Our team coaching can help, but there is an approach that I think you might want to learn. As it happens, I have a colleague who loves to teach teams how to find a Both/And when they are used to thinking in either-or terms. Barry is an expert in an approach called Polarity Thinking, something that I am just beginning to feel a sense of mastery for. Would you like to meet him?"

"I don't think we can afford not to," Ted said soberly. "When can he get here? And can Edgar join us too so it gets integrated into the work he's doing with us?"

"That's a great idea," agreed Jordan. "As a matter of fact, Edgar knows my colleague too. They are both experts in sustainability."

31

COULD WE BOTH BE RIGHT?

Everyone scanned the unusual setup as they filed into the meeting room, curious about what they'd be doing. The flip charts around the room weren't unexpected—the SLT and Edgar often did brainstorming. However, the painters' tape of a 2 × 2 grid on the floor had them perplexed. A loop of string wound across the 4 quadrants in a sideways figure 8 was an added puzzle.

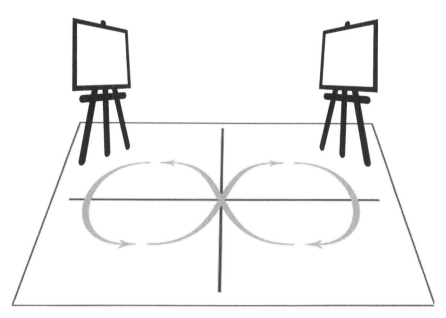

Jordan welcomed everybody, inviting them to be seated. She began the session by introducing the man seated next to her. "This is Barry Johnson, the colleague I told you about who is an expert on polarity thinking."[16] She gestured toward Barry, who acknowledged their welcome. Then Jordan continued by asking the team an opening question: "Is it better for a leader to be humble or to be confident?"

"Confident!" shouted Arun, echoed by Donna. "Humble," suggested Patrick.

Jordan continued with a second question. "Should you focus on the short term or on the long term?"

"Long term," said Jack. "Definitely long term," Ted, Edgar, and Lynn concurred. Donna and Arun looked unsure, while Patrick tentatively suggested "Both?"

"Okay, here's an easy one," Jordan suggested. "As a leader, is it preferable to advocate for your own perspective or to inquire into what others think?"

"Advocate!" shouted Arun, Lynn, and Jack simultaneously. Ted offered, "Inquire?" with a question in his voice, while Donna, Edgar, and Patrick shook their heads, making no response.

Enjoying the mood of curiosity, Jordan paused as she looked around the team.

"Come on, Jordan! What are the right answers?" Arun pressured their long-term team coach.

Jordan answered Arun quickly, "To tell you the right answers, I'd like to invite Barry to share something with you that has been his life's work—Polarity Thinking. I believe that what we will be sharing with you today is one of the answers to how the leaders at Tech Environments can help one another and the company to thrive in a VUCA world. It's an 'us' kind of approach, as in 'How could we both be right?'" At this, Jordan gestured to Barry, inviting him to take the lead.

As he took center stage, Barry began, "Jordan just asked you some unfair questions. I want to reassure each of you that no matter how you responded, you were right." Barry waited for Arun to finish cheering before continuing. "And, no matter which of the two options you chose, your response was inadequate, incomplete, and will ultimately lead to failure." Now Barry had to tolerate a scowl from Arun before going on. "The truth is that in each of these pairs—confidence and humility, short term and long term, advocacy and inquiry—the two need each other to yield sustainable results. A leader can't be successful by choosing only one; you have to embody both to succeed over the long haul."

"So what you are saying," Donna said, "is that choosing between them is always the wrong option?"

"Yes," Barry responded. "It *is* a wrong choice to pick between the competing options, and to believe your selection is adequate all by itself. Just as an example: if you always focused on the external customers and never on your internal team, that would result in failure for Tech Environments. But it's not that you got the answer wrong—because on the other hand, if you always focused on the internal team and never considered your customers, that choice too would result in failure. The only way to generate sustainable success is to recognize that both your internal team and your external customers are vitally important. This is the essence of polarity thinking. A polarity is an interdependent pair of values, strategies, or objectives where both are necessary; neither choice alone is sufficient. Polarity thinking is indispensable in complex situations where either-or thinking and traditional problem solving won't do. Jordan invited me to join you because the challenges you are faced with require you to embrace a Both/And approach that enables you to leverage your diverse perspectives." Now Barry looked expectantly around the room, inviting their input.

"I sort of understand," Patrick commented. "But can you make it a little clearer?"

Barry answered eagerly, "I'll do better than that, Patrick. We'll experience a polarity together and you can see how it works. I call it mapping when we use the process of fully exploring a polarity. For the sake of having a map that you can immediately see the value of, let's use a pair of competing objectives that Jordan tells me you have been struggling with: stability and innovation. And to map this polarity, I'll ask you all to get up and join me here on this setup I've taped on the floor. As you can see, the tape creates four quadrants. I'm putting the word 'stability' on the horizontal for the left side of the map and the word 'innovation' on the right side. We can tell the top of the map because the words are right side up when we are facing correctly. I invite you all to join me and stand in the top left-hand quadrant of this 2 × 2 polarity map we have on the floor. This is the quadrant we will call the upside of stability. What is the upside of stability?" Barry looked expectantly at the group.

"Consistency," suggested Lynn.

"Clients count on knowing what to expect," said Ted.

"Comfort," offered Jack.

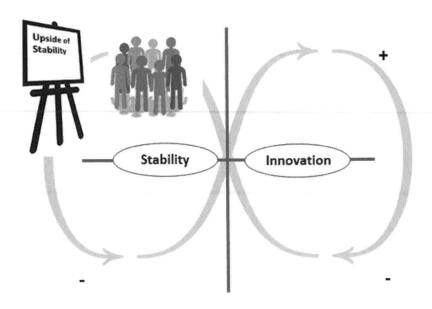

"Good," affirmed Barry. "It's easy for you to see the upsides of stability, of keeping things the way they are. So here is a challenge I have for you: What happens if you come to believe that stability is the right answer and you neglect the need for innovation? What is the downside of stability you'll experience if you think that's all you need?"

"Outdated products," commented Donna.

"Boredom," added Arun. "And our clients would go looking for more innovative vendors. I think that's where we were six months ago. That's when that horrible article was published in *Tech Consulting Review*. That's what made our team focus on innovation again."

Barry then pointed out the string infinity loop on the floor that no one had paid any attention to. "A polarity has a natural flow. Every polarity works the same. You get the upside of your preferred pole, in this case stability for several of you. But if you stay focused on that pole and don't also consciously attend to innovation, then over time you'll experience stability's downside. When you do, you'll naturally move to the other pole to get its benefits. In this case, you might brainstorm some cutting-edge products and include them in client solutions, which could help both your clients and your team feel excited. Is that what you've been doing, Arun?"

Arun quickly nodded, "Yes, we nudged some of our most creative developers, and they started working on some ideas they hadn't taken time to prototype yet. It's been exciting!"

Barry smiled. "I can see you've enjoyed refocusing on innovation, Arun. Of course, if you decided that innovation was the only right answer and that you should avoid stability in the future, you'd experience the downside of innovation. Overfocusing on innovation would result in what?"

"That's a no-brainer for me," asserted Lynn. "When you always innovate and neglect the need for any stability, you get too many poorly developed products. The products have a lot of bugs, and clients don't understand them because new products are coming so quickly that no one has time to learn how to use them effectively. And instead of our team having a sense of energy, they get exhausted."

Even Arun nodded his head thoughtfully as Barry noted on a flip chart all of these downsides of an overfocus on innovation to the neglect of stability.

"Absolutely," agreed Barry. "As you can see, you have been following this infinity loop. You experienced the downside of focusing on stability for too long and you moved to focusing on innovation. What I will predict, however, is that if you decide innovation is the right answer and you disregard the value of stability, then you will begin to get feedback at some point in the future that you need to adjust and focus some of your effort on creating stability again and not solely on innovating new products."

Thirty minutes into the exercise, having moved around the grid and explored each of the four quadrants' qualities, Arun looked at Ted in surprise. "I guess I should say thanks, Ted. It turns out I need you after all. You help me understand the benefits of stability."

"Ditto," Ted replied. "I had no idea each of us was seeing just half the picture. I thought we had to keep debating until we landed on the right answer. What we're learning about with Barry here suggests that we need to listen to each other instead, and to consciously move back and forth between stability and innovation. The more we do that mindfully and proactively, the better."

"I can definitely see how this helps us with VUCA," Lynn observed. "We can't avoid volatility. However, seeing it this way could help us to anticipate what will happen, and to take action before it's too late. Having a process like this also helps us organize the complexity instead of being confused by multiple right answers."

"I think you've got it!" Jordan affirmed. "This is what I was telling you about—a way to get the best of both, to value your different perspectives and work as a team instead of letting differences cause you stress and conflict."

"So now I'm curious," said Patrick. "Is this what happens with Donna and me when she wants to focus on our results and I believe we have to pay attention to our people?"

Before Jordan or Barry could respond, Lynn interrupted, "Or what happens with Jack and me when I want to avoid risk, and he is concerned about being so risk-averse that we don't challenge ourselves to grow?"

"Or when Edgar wants to plan, and I just want us to execute?" Arun asked.

Everyone laughed at all the polarities that were obvious to them now.

Barry smiled. "You're absolutely right—polarities are everywhere in our complex world. Whenever you feel a tension between two competing perspectives, when smart people are backing both sides, and especially when you end up having the same arguments repeatedly, chances are you've got a polarity. Once you recognize that, you can engage everyone in mapping the upsides and downsides of both poles, the way we just did, to see the situation more clearly and completely."

Jordan applauded the team, before turning to thank Barry. "I told you, Barry, that they would get it. They are more than ready to find a different way. Thank you for sharing your work with us." Barry smiled and nodded.

32

TEAMS HELP EACH OTHER

After the success and momentum of their polarity-mapping conversation with Jordan and Barry, the SLT felt more relaxed and confident. They had decided to take some time and think about what they'd experienced instead of taking immediate action. Monday morning would come soon enough.

Monday mornings were planning time for the SLT, always accompanied by coffee, tea, and breakfast. As everyone filled plates with fruit and bagels, they caught up on families and weekend activities.

Jack had a request. "Any ideas for me? My wife says that I need to choose a gift for our daughter's graduation. We are giving her a two-week trip to Germany with a couple of her friends. But my wife suggested something personal from me."

"What does she like?" asked Patrick.

"Her friends, of course, and she actually loves time with family. The reason she chose Germany for her trip is because her cousin is living there while he goes to school. She also loves art and music. Any ideas?" Jack glanced around.

"Would she want to spend time just with you, Jack? Is there a way to turn that into a gift?" suggested Donna.

Ted agreed, and added, "What's something the two of you would enjoy doing?"

"We like to travel together," Jack said. "We had a great time visiting a couple of graduate schools she applied to. The campuses were fun to explore, and we are both foodies so we enjoyed trying some new restaurants. But my wife was suggesting something I could wrap up and give to our daughter."

"I'd be happy to help you create some kind of a brochure and gift basket with clues to experiences you could have while sharing a day together," offered Donna. "I love doing that kind of thing, and it's a big hit when we do gifts like that for our best clients. Plus, that would ensure you have something tangible to give her."

"I appreciate your offer, Donna, and gratefully accept. It will give me a good opportunity to see you in your element creating too. Thanks." Jack nodded his appreciation. As he organized his papers for the meeting, Jack realized something he hadn't noticed before. *This is a far cry from the conversations we were having not so long ago*, he thought. *Just being able to have an easy exchange—I guess that's one clear indication we are making strides in our team. It's certainly more pleasant to start our week this way. Here's hoping it pays off in our business.*

33

CAN OUR FAMILIES GET
IN ON THE DEAL?

A few days later, Edgar was beginning his day in a coffee shop. *This is one of those things I like about being a consultant*, Edgar thought, *meeting people for coffee. Donna says this place is her favorite. Meeting here means we won't get interrupted. I wonder what she has been thinking about the possibility of us doing a community outreach program on bullying. Marianne has got our internal bullying initiative moving forward, but it would be great to take it external.* Picturing his son Josh, Edgar found himself reflective. *Will Donna go for what Josh is suggesting—a "Find Something to Do Besides Bullying" program co-facilitated by teens and by Tech Environments' team members? Josh is so excited and determined. I hate to see him disappointed. But will Donna think it's a good idea?* Scanning the café for a table, Edgar wondered. *Should I just order for both of us? After all, everyone knows Donna's favorite latte.* A tap on the shoulder gave Edgar his answer.

"My son Josh wants to help," Edgar blurted out as soon as he saw Donna.

Donna laughed, "Good to see you too, Edgar. Can I get some caffeine on board so I can process what you are even talking about?"

"Oh, sure. I didn't really mean to start that way. Coffee is a good idea. Guess I am just preoccupied with something Josh asked me to speak with you about." Edgar looked slightly embarrassed.

As the two waited in line, they made small talk about how Edgar's move to his new home was going, and how his daughter and his son Josh were adjusting to their schools. Donna had just returned from a conference, and shared a few experiences with the marketing folks she'd spent the past few days with. As they sat down with their coffees, she began, "Speaking of the reason we are meeting this morning, I floated the anti-bullying community outreach idea to a few of my colleagues. All of them fell completely in love with it. They were impressed that our interest in a bullying initiative came from our own Tech Environments' experiences in needing to address the bully problem at work. In marketing talk, they said that made us 'relatable.'"

"Josh wants to help," Edgar repeated. "He has this idea that it needs to come from the kids themselves. We can support them, of course, but he thinks it'll have more impact if it comes from them. Josh even has a name for the program: 'Find Something to Do Besides Bullying.' From what he's experienced being bullied himself, Josh is convinced that most bullies pick on others because they don't have anything better to do. He says that most bullies aren't bad people; they just don't feel very good about themselves, and they take it out on others." Edgar glanced at Donna to gauge her reaction.

"Find Something to Do Besides Bullying!" Donna exclaimed. "I love the name. It doesn't blame the bully, but it does hold them accountable. And I can imagine how it might enable everyone to be part of the solution—the bully finds something else to do, but bystanders can offer options, and victims of bullies can get help from friends, parents, and teachers in finding bullies something better to do. Bullies will get the message: there are better things to do." Smiling, Donna tapped her paper latte cup to Edgar's in a mock toast to celebrate the idea.

"It's a wonderful idea for the kids, Edgar. Putting on my marketing hat for a moment, it's a valuable opportunity for Tech Environments too. A program like 'Find Something to Do Besides Bullying' doesn't look or feel like schmoozing to get business; it is a way to be an integral part of our community, all while addressing a big issue in our schools. What's next?"

34

HOLDING ON,
AND LETTING GO

Back here again! We sure do spend a lot of time together, Edgar observed as the SLT settled into their seats around the conference table for their next weekly meeting. Edgar had volunteered to facilitate the gathering, taking advantage of Jack's desire to divvy up the leadership load with his team. *Jack's experience with Ellie the horse has really changed his commitment to shared leadership,* Edgar reflected. *It's a good opportunity to experience and learn from our different styles. I'll have to remember to use this same approach with other clients.*

Once everyone had arrived, Edgar initiated the focus of the meeting. "Jack tells me his agenda for today is anything that will keep moving us forward toward this sustainably successful company we are striving to be," Edgar stated. "As you all know, many things are improving around here. Our business pipeline is more robust than it has been, technology publications are finally giving us some positive press for the work we are doing with our clients, and Patrick says that no team members have jumped ship recently." More seriously, Edgar continued, "Still, I think the seven of us have some work to do as individual leaders. I thought we'd focus today on ourselves instead of Tech Environments as a whole. After all, sustainability doesn't happen without the leadership being on board. As this company's senior team, others expect us to be good, and to keep getting better. I have an idea about some commitments we can make on that improvement journey, intentions we can hold one another accountable for."

Jack interrupted with a quick, "Now don't get too carried away, Edgar, it's just one meeting. . . ."

Edgar laughed easily, "I think one meeting may be all we need to get started, Jack. I suspect you will all find that what I'm inviting you to do is something you've already been considering. This will just give you a chance to verbalize it in front of all of us."

"Okay, I'm all ears," Jack agreed. Around him, everyone else seemed attentive, which Edgar took as a sign to continue.

Edgar now stood up. "All right, so here's what I've been thinking about. You remember the session that Jordan and Barry did with us on polarities, aka 'Both/And thinking'? Remember how there are certain polarities that all leaders need to pay attention to? Some of Jordan's examples were humility and confidence, and task and relationship. Ringing any bells?" Edgar scanned the group.

Seeing the nods, Edgar went on. "There's a polarity I've been thinking about personally that I believe all of us would benefit from becoming more aware of—it's holding on and letting go."

Arun spoke up, "Sounds interesting, Edgar, but isn't that just the same as stability and change? Stability is holding on and change is letting go, right?"

Edgar appreciated the question. "Yes, I agree, Arun. They are very similar. Framing it in this way, as holding on and letting go, personalizes it for me as a leader. With stability and change, I tend to focus on the organization and our strategy. When I think about holding on and letting go, it's easier for me to recognize how I might take action as a leader and role model for others." Edgar glanced at Arun, noting that he appeared to accept the explanation.

Edgar now put on his teacher's hat to remind the others of what they'd learned about polarities. "So just a brief recap then—when we are talking about a polarity, it always involves two interdependent objectives or values, both of which are necessary to long-term success and sustainability. Both poles have upsides, or benefits, and of course they both have downsides too when we overfocus on one and neglect the other. To make this specific, if I ask you about the benefits or upsides of holding on, what do you experience when you hold on?"

Several weighed in all at once,

"Consistency!"

"Comfort, a sense of ease."

"Familiarity."

"Trustworthiness."

Edgar quickly jotted down their responses in the 2 × 2 table he'd drawn on the flip chart. Then he redirected the group, "And what if you always hold on, ignore the letting go pole, and never let go of anything? What will you experience then?"

"Clutter."

"Boredom, for me," Arun admitted.

"Complacency!"

"Stagnation," Ted added.

"Brilliant," Edgar affirmed. "So then naturally, if you were experiencing all those negative impacts of holding on, you'd move to the other pole and begin to let go of some things. What benefit would that have for you as a leader?"

"Space for new ideas."

"Space in general. I'd let go of material stuff too," Lynn offered.

"Excitement about not knowing what might take its place."

"Energy."

"Curiosity."

Edgar jotted down their ideas above the words "Letting Go" on the map. "Again, you're doing a wonderful job articulating the benefits of letting go. You can see why we might overfocus on letting go once we start. Letting go has a lot of benefits. But what would happen if we believed that we had landed on the right answer and we focused only on letting go, never holding on to anything?" Edgar inquired.

"Inconsistency."

"Too much space. Emptiness."

"Anxiety, and others would catch it and become anxious as well," Jack suggested.

"Uncertainty too."

As Edgar completed the polarity map, the senior leaders gazed up at it.

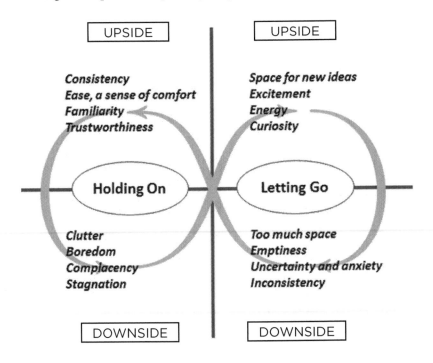

"Wow, we are getting good at this," Donna commented. "Polarity mapping seemed complicated when Jordan and Barry initially shared it, but it gets easier every time we do it. And just like the first time we did it, mapping the whole picture by filling in the four quadrants makes it clear why both poles are important. Even if I prefer letting go and doing something new, I'd never choose to do *only* that when I see the benefits of holding on."

"Excellent!" Edgar appreciated Donna's willingness to acknowledge her own preference, and its limitations. "Everyone else on board?" Seeing nods all around, Edgar persisted, "Now I'm going to up the ante for each of you, and ask you to reflect for a few minutes and jot down what you personally are committed to holding on to as we take this next step as a company, and what you are ready to let go of. I've passed around some low-tech index cards—green on one side and orange on the other so you can capture your commitments. Let's take ten minutes so each of you has a chance to consider."

The next few minutes found the room silent except for the scratch of pens and the flipping over of index cards. Finally, Edgar called time. "Who wants to start?"

"I'll go," Lynn volunteered. "I'm not sure if I did this right, but here is what I wrote down. I intend to hold on to my commitment to intentionally manage risk. That's my job, after all. However, I think I'd be a more effective leader if I let go of my habit of blaming others when mistakes happen. I'm not sure that is really helpful."

"Thanks for starting us off with a bang, Lynn. That is exactly what I had in mind. Who else?" Edgar encouraged.

Patrick immediately shared his: "I'm going to let go of needing to be perfect, since it's not possible in any case. And I'm going to hold on to continuous learning."

Arun stood up and declared, "You all will be happy to know I'm going to work on letting go of thinking I'm the only one with the right answer, and I'm going to hold on to high standards for our products and services."

Donna went next. "I'm holding on to paying attention to the numbers and growing our reputation. I'd like to let go of cramming my schedule so full that I fail to keep my promises. I'm going to need your help with that," she added.

Edgar smiled. "This will be a much different team, and company, if you each follow through on those commitments. Jack? Ted?"

"I'm near the end of my career," Ted commented. "So I'm in a little different place than the rest of you. When I think of adding value at this stage, I believe I need to hold on to my willingness to mentor and guide others. I'll try to let go of being overly focused on my finance team. I think that has sometimes led to silos and drama in the past."

Jack looked pensive. "When I went to the equine coach, the horse taught me a lot about letting go of the need to be in control. I'll keep working on letting go of that. Related to that, I'm going to hold on to trust and believing that people generally have positive intentions, even when things don't work out. I think doing those two things will help me be a more inspiring and approachable leader."

Edgar had been busy recording all their answers, but now stopped to offer his own. "I am going to hold on to my commitment to offer appreciation and recognition on a frequent basis. I enjoy doing it, but it's easy not to bother with it when things are going well. I am going to let go of needing to know exactly what's next. Uncertainty is the hardest part of VUCA for me. Since I can't always know what's next, I'll trust I'll be ready for it, whatever it is." Edgar added his own vows to the list and stood back to examine it.

	Holding On	**Letting Go**
Lynn	Commitment to intentionally manage risk	Habit of blaming others when mistakes happen
Patrick	Continuous learning	Needing to be perfect
Arun	High standards for our services and products	Thinking I'm the only one with the right answer
Donna	Attention to the numbers and growing our reputation	Cramming my schedule so full that I fail to keep my promises
Ted	Willingness to mentor and guide others	Being overly focused on my finance team
Jack	Trust, believing that each person has positive intentions	The need to be in control
Edgar	Offer appreciation and recognition on a frequent basis	Needing to know what's next

"What do you all think? Valuable use of an hour?" Edgar inquired of the rest of the team.

"Not bad, Edgar. Not bad at all," Lynn affirmed. "I'm appreciating you being back more every day."

35

SOMETIMES THE "US" IS A HORSE

To many of the leaders, it seemed like the strangest use of their time—to leave Tech Environments and go to a farm to spend an entire day with horses. However, Jack had been insistent on the value of equine coaching. He'd explained that horses are uniquely attuned to the energy we give off, and offer a unique way to practice being in relationship with someone different from yourself—in this case, a horse. Given the power of his own experience with a horse, Jack had invited twenty of the leaders at Tech Environments to participate in a horse-assisted leadership session.

The equine coach Marge and Tech Environments' Coach Jordan had helped leaders to identify their individual leadership goals ahead of time. Those on the SLT chose their holding-on or letting-go commitments—Lynn wanted to practice letting go of her tendency to blame others and Patrick was embracing a new mode of learning. The next tier of leaders had identified a wide range of goals, including increased confidence, building trust, and developing executive presence.

When the group arrived at the horse farm, Jack saw that the setup for a team coaching session was different. There were two equine coaches and two rings. One enclosure was a small one like the one Jack and the mare Ellie had experienced. The other pen was a large oval, with boards and barrels in an arrangement that looked like an obstacle course. Jack had decided to be a spectator at the team ring, respecting individual leaders' privacy when working one-on-one with a horse. As Marge introduced the team to one of the horses they'd be working with, Jack noticed that several of the leaders were obviously nervous. *It's no wonder they are nervous,* he thought. *I only had to get Ellie to follow me. Their task is a lot harder than mine was.*

Marge directed the team to guide a horse named Lewis through the obstacles, all without touching the horse or his halter. While Jack observed, he realized how much of this task was about how the team communicated with one another, as well as how they built trust with the horse. *If they can work together at something this challenging,* he thought, *there's no doubt in my mind that they'll be more effective with our clients.* So far, however, the team looked woefully inept, waving their arms at Lewis and watching him trot away from them to the other end of the ring. *I'm not sure I'd be doing any better in their shoes,* Jack thought. As he listened to the questions the equine coach asked his team, Jack saw some of the leaders beginning to nod as they recognized that they'd have to collaborate and work together.

When Lynn, Pete, and Arun talked about it later, they couldn't seem to agree on what had transpired. One moment, the horse pen had been filled with clouds of dust and the sound of people's voices and a cantering horse. Chaos. The next moment, all movement and sound seemed suspended in time. And then, everything had returned to normal. Back to normal, except that suddenly, the horse was taking his lead from the Tech Environments team, and everyone was looking at each other trying to figure out how they had made that happen. Because something had changed for sure. Just minutes before, the team had looked, and felt, silly and unskilled. The leaders had been waving their arms and the lengths of rope they held in frustration while the horse seemed to be laughing at, or simply ignoring, them. And then, unexpectedly, the three leaders and the horse in the ring with them were working together. The team was clear about what they wanted the horse to do, and communicating smoothly in their roles as teammates. They were relying on one another, and Lewis seemed to recognize their leadership. It was like night and day, as if some transformation had occurred. The team still wasn't quite sure why or how they had begun to jell.

Yet something clearly clicked for them, Jack mused later. Because in the weeks that followed, there was a tangibly altered vibe in the air around Tech Environments too. The individuals who'd shared in the equine coaching experience seemed to be functioning better, more comfortable in their own skin and more fluid in their execution as a team. Pete acted more confident, even in very large groups and with senior leaders. Arun seemed uncharacteristically open to input, and much less self-absorbed. Lynn, who'd admitted she was terrified of horses, was talking about the value of taking risks in situations of uncertainty. *And all their progress makes me more willing to let go,* Jack thought, *and much more sure of the team. That's kind of nice.*

And Pete, Arun, and Lynn weren't the only ones. It seemed as if almost every person who'd attended the day with the horses had come away with exactly what they needed to be more effective as a leader.[17] Jack had been right about that for sure. The horses weren't just helpful to someone like him, someone who loved to be in control. Equine coaching seemed equally beneficial to an emerging leader who was uncertain and tentative. The horses seemed to understand what was needed.

And speaking of what is needed, Jack considered the day's schedule. *What I need to be doing right now is heading into our team meeting.*

36

CAN OUR TEAMS HELP US?

A*nother meeting!* Ted invariably found himself adding up all the salaries in the room for any meeting. If he added in the missed revenue generation, he knew he'd drive himself crazy. These gatherings represented a big commitment—pulling everyone from their regular jobs to meet. *I guess breaking my habit of focusing on cost is not as easy as I'd hoped,* Ted thought. *What was it we learned from that Empowerment Dynamic*[18] *stuff about a problem focus and an outcome focus? Something like when I'm focused on the problem, I'll act out of fear? Focusing on problems will tend to make me feel like a victim. When I notice that, I'm supposed to shift my thinking. How do I do that again? Oh, that's right—ask myself "What do I want?" Aspirations. Okay, that's not so hard. Let's see, I want the investment in this meeting to pay off. That's better.* Feeling slightly better, Ted sat down between Jen and Javy, two of his finance team members who he expected to be future leaders at Tech Environments. Jen nodded at their boss, and both continued tapping on their smartphones, probably answering emails while they waited for the session to start. *No wasted time there,* Ted noted.

While he had a few minutes, Ted looked at the flip chart pages he'd stuck up around the room with their one-word titles—Values. Us.

Curiosity. Aspirations. *Those words make me optimistic,* he thought. *Focusing my attention on those four concepts is what brings me to work every day. I wonder what everyone else will think.*

Ted distributed copies of a financial report for everyone to review, then summarized its key points efficiently. He concluded the report by projecting the final table on the screen.

Issue	Strategic tool	Lead(s)	Budget	Actual to date
Volatility	Values-based leadership	Jack	$89,000	$43,545 (48.9%)
Uncertainty	Us before Me	Lynn & Ted	$55,000	$12,391 (22.5%)
Complexity	Creating a Curiosity Culture	Patrick & Arun	$180,000	$70,017 (38.9%)
Ambiguity	Aspirational focus	Donna & Edgar	$95,000	$9,928 (10.5%)

"As you can see, we're spending down our budget to address each of the four components of VUCA. Any thoughts about our approach?" The members of the SLT gazed up at the image, but no one commented. Ted challenged them, "What do you notice?" He waited, then nudged them again, "For a smart group of people, I'm surprised you don't see it."

"Ummm. Jack's spending money faster than the rest of us?" Edgar ventured.

Ted shook his head.

Donna suggested, "Patrick and Arun have the biggest budget?"

Ted nodded. "Yes, but we already knew culture change would cost a chunk of money this year. That's nothing new. Come on! If I see it, I know you must." He waited semi-patiently as they studied the table.

"Ahh, I think I've got it," smiled Jack.

"Me too!" shouted Arun and Lynn at the same time.

Patrick and Donna continued to look perplexed. Ted finally took pity on them. "Our four strategic tools—they start with the same letters as VUCA. We've spelled out VUCA with our strategic plan."

"Wow," said Patrick. "VUCA for VUCA. That is very cool. If we had planned it, I'd say it was brilliant."

"It's interesting," asserted Arun. "But won't people get confused? I mean, we've been talking about VUCA as a threat to Tech Environments. Everyone will be baffled if we start describing VUCA as a solution."

"I think you're right, Arun. The symmetry between problem and solution is compelling. I love that it spells out VUCA. But we do need to find a way to differentiate our solution strategy from VUCA itself." Jack echoed Arun's concern. "Maybe you have an idea, Donna? What would we call this if we were marketing it to our internal team?"

"What about 'Tools'? Donna responded. "These are all tools we are using to respond to VUCA. VUCA tools for a VUCA world. It's kind of catchy, and it'll make it easy for everyone to remember."

"And we often talk about building your leadership toolkit," Patrick added. "VUCA tools definitely does that!"

"VUCA tools," Jack mused. "I like it too. Thanks, Ted, for noticing it. Your perspective is one of the things that makes me grateful you've stuck around Tech Environments instead of retiring. Well, that and the fact that you keep our books balanced. That makes me grateful too." Laughing, Jack brought the meeting to a close, enjoying the moment.

As Ted left the conference room, he reflected on how obsessed with cost he'd been as the meeting began. *I have to admit that this was well worth our time,* he thought. *We are creating something enduring here. I guess you can't always put a price on that.*

37

FIND SOMETHING TO DO BESIDES BULLYING

As he pulled in to the high school parking lot, Edgar was reflective. *Work often takes away from our families*, he thought. *I'm glad to have the rare opportunity to combine the two this afternoon.*

Edgar and his son Josh hadn't had many opportunities to work together, but they were excited to be the main agenda item for today's high school assembly. The two had spent time preparing what they wanted to say, but Edgar deferred to his son to take the lead. After all, it was Josh's school, his idea, and putting an end to bullying had become Josh's passion. Father and son both felt more than a little nervous sitting side by side on the stage, as Principal Nellie McIntosh prepared to introduce them. *There are few things scarier than looking out at an auditorium of a thousand teenagers*, Edgar reflected. He shifted again in his seat. *We'll see how all this goes. I hope Josh is not as nervous as I am.*

Ms. McIntosh stood up and brought the auditorium to attention. "I am aware that this next hour is all that stands between you and the end of the school day. I think you will be pleasantly surprised that today's assembly includes one of your own as a speaker, and will also feature a business leader from the community. Let me introduce to all of you Josh Mienz, a member of our first-year class, and his father, Edgar Mienz, who is a sustainability consultant, currently working with Tech Environments here in town. Please join me in welcoming Josh and his father, Mr. Mienz. I ask that you give them your full attention as they talk about something that is important to all of us."

Josh got up quickly and replaced his principal at the podium. *He doesn't look nervous at all*, Edgar marveled. *He has really grown up.*

Josh surprised the assembly by beginning with an announcement. "Some of you are bullies," he asserted, pointedly looking around at faces in the audience. "You think I don't know that, but I do. You know it too."

"Some of you are being bullied," Josh continued. "And you too might think no one knows about it, that you are in it alone. Nothing could be further from the truth. You are not alone."

"And many of you," now Josh gestured at the entire audience. "Are bully enablers. You aren't bullies yourself, but you allow it to happen. I get it—you are hoping not to be the next target. But you are to blame for the bullying just as much as the next person."

The restlessness in the audience had ceased as students seemed riveted by where Josh was going with this. *I'm not sure myself what he'll say*, Edgar thought. *How much is he going to reveal about what he went through?*

Josh now stared out at the crowd, and asked a question, "Which one do you think I was? Was I a bully, a not-so-innocent witness to bullying, or was I a bully's victim?" He scanned the audience and they stared back at him, taking in Josh's slender 5'9" frame, his obvious confidence, and his question.

"Okay, a show of hands—how many of you think I was the bully?" A third of the audience raised their hands.

"A bully enabler?" Josh asked. Half the attendees shot up their hands.

"And how many of you think I was bullied, that I was the one being abused?" A few tentative hands were raised.

"Bingo!" said Josh seriously. "When I was in middle school, right here in this town, I was the victim of bullies. And I reacted in the worst possible way. I tried to keep it a secret until it was nearly too late. I've invited my dad here today to tell you about what happened. Dad?"

Here goes, thought Edgar. *I can't let him down now.* Edgar rose from his chair and looked out at the teens in front of him. He approached the mic, and took a deep breath before beginning. "There is a phone call that no father ever wants to receive," Edgar said somberly. "Three years ago, I got a call from Josh's school. The voice on the line informed me that my son was on his way to the emergency room. By the time I had rushed to the hospital, Josh's stomach had been pumped, and he was in the intensive care unit. His mother and I spent a frightening night not knowing if Josh would survive." Recognizing that many of the students looked upset and some were wiping their eyes, Edgar continued. "As you can see, Josh did survive, and he has become one of the strongest people I know. We moved away from here after that happened because I wanted Josh to get a fresh start in a new place. We made a home there, and Josh recovered, but we all missed living here. It was Josh's idea to move back, and he convinced our family to do so. It takes a lot of courage for us to stand here in front of you and share our story. The reason is that Josh cares about each one of you, his high school classmates, and wants to make sure that you know what to do about bullying."

Later, both Josh and Edgar were glad that several teachers had taken video of their presentation on smartphones. Neither father nor son could recollect exactly what they had said, but both remembered the many eager questions, and the standing ovation when they had finished sharing the "Do Something Besides Bullying" program. They also recalled that every hand in the audience had shot up when Josh asked who was committed to ending bullying. Josh was beyond ecstatic at the response. *It's been a long journey,* Edgar thought, *and I am amazed it's taken us to this place and time. I'm so thankful that Tech Environments was willing to support us in making this happen. It means the world to Josh, and to me.*

38

EDGAR WONDERS WHAT THE RIGHT CHOICE IS

A few weeks after the high school assembly, Edgar was headed for Patrick's office. *Wow!* he thought. *Things have really come full circle in a way I never expected. When I came back here with my family, I hoped that Tech Environments would want me as a sustainability consultant. I knew that they were in trouble. Fast-forward to now, when it seems that they want me to become an employee again, part of the senior leadership team. I wonder if that's the right choice. I hope Patrick can be objective enough to help me think this through.* By now Edgar had arrived at Patrick's workplace. Edgar greeted Marianne in the adjacent office before tapping on Patrick's door.

Patrick got up to greet Edgar with a warm handshake. "Good to see you, Edgar. I'm excited to have this conversation. You looked startled when we told you that we are interested in having you as a permanent member of the team again."

Edgar agreed. "I am surprised, Patrick. When my family and I moved back to town, I knew I could help Tech Environments. If I wasn't confident of the value I bring, I would never have offered you two months of my services for free," Edgar said, recalling how he'd convinced Tech Environments to "hire" him.

"Yes, at the time I thought you were crazy to do that, but by a month into our work with you, everyone was convinced we needed your sustainability expertise. It was a good move on your part to remove the financial barrier and make it easy for us. Otherwise Ted would have balked at the cost," Patrick acknowledged.

"So, what makes you think Tech Environments still needs me?" Edgar asked. "After all, you are right where you hoped to be. And it's easier to let a consultant go than to get rid of an employee. I'd be out of integrity as a sustainability expert if I didn't mention that."

"We are in good shape, Edgar, and we'd like to stay that way. We appreciate your dynamic presence on the senior leadership team. Everyone likes you, and we all trust you. You are experienced, and you have good judgment. Ted had his doubts initially, but even he can see that the cost of hiring you full-time will be more than offset by the value you bring. Lynn appreciates having you as an ally in risk reduction. And she doesn't even remotely experience you as a threat, despite your being in her role before you left Tech Environments the first time." Patrick was in full recruitment mode now.

Edgar looked unconvinced. "My family loves the idea of my working here again, but I'm not so sure. I enjoy the variety I get consulting. I'd miss that. And, to be honest, I'm not sure you need me here full-time."

"If not full-time, would you consider a fractional role?" Patrick persisted. "We haven't had fractional leaders on the SLT before, but I know a lot of other companies are doing it. And I recall you've held a fractional role as Chief Sustainability Officer for at least one company."

Edgar nodded, and waited for Patrick to continue.

Patrick obliged. "The position we would like to offer you is COO. As you know, Arun is currently acting both as our Chief Technology Officer and COO. He's had a tough time balancing both and is eager to give up the COO role. Having you in that position would be an ideal transition, a way to fortify our team with your experience. Would you consider signing on half-time, so you'd still have time for other temporary gigs as a consultant?"

"You are a hard man to turn down," Edgar said with a grin.

"That's what I hear," Patrick responded. "Is that a yes?"

"It's a yes, assuming that the SLT is unanimous in their support for the role. I'd love to be a permanent member of the team again." Edgar smiled, shaking his head in disbelief. "Thanks, Patrick. I'm delighted."

"Me too!" Patrick agreed.

39

CELEBRATING OUR SUCCESSES

The private room at one of their favorite restaurants offered a pleasant setting for the SLT's annual review and celebration dinner. Arun began the brief presentation portion of the meeting. He displayed an image from his laptop for the others on the senior leadership team to see. "Bottom-line results this year: I believe we've addressed the talent pipeline issue by becoming an internship site for two local university technology programs and one executive graduate program. Two students have already indicated their plans to apply for positions here following graduation. On the technology and business development front, we have several promising new products in development. Our clients feel we are being both innovative and realistic. We don't offer them crazy projections like the one in this recent report on artificial intelligence saying that AI robots will be serving on boards of directors by the year 2026.[19] We are getting better all the time in creating smart technologies, but even I am not arrogant enough to claim that we can create a robot who's better than a thinking, feeling human being."

"Wait a minute, Arun," Lynn interrupted. "Did you just actually say that feelings are important? What dimension have I wandered into?"

Jordan entered as the room erupted in laughter. She looked around at the group, enjoying the moment with them. "Last year I would never have guessed the time would come that I'd walk into a room at Tech Environments and find its senior leaders laughing," Jordan exclaimed. "Crying, yes, but certainly not laughing. You have definitely inspired me with your resilience, and the hard work you've done on yourselves and your company, this year. Thank you for including me in your celebration."

Patrick acknowledged Jordan's role in the turnaround. "You are being too kind, Jordan. As you remember, we were a mess. No doubt about that. And, to your credit, you didn't try to fix us. Instead you coached us to be better leaders, to lead ourselves and one another forward in the midst of the chaos. You made VUCA approachable with your steady presence and your willingness to hold us accountable for being as good as we wanted to be."

Jack gazed around at his team and reflected on the last year. *It has been a whirlwind. I can't even fathom how much progress we've made,* he thought. *From VUCA to VUCA Tools to thriving. It's been quite a journey. Hearing what everyone is saying today is a powerful reminder of how far we've come.*

Patrick and Lynn went next, doing a tag-team presentation of the success of TE's people initiatives. The pair highlighted the anti-bullying program inside the company. Efforts to address harassment and bullying had resulted in Tech Environments being recognized by the National Bullying Prevention Center. Even more important, there was evidence of the impact in reduced grievances and more positive online reviews. Tech Environments had recently achieved status on Glassdoor.com as an Employees' Choice. Lynn and Patrick both felt a deep sense of satisfaction in all they'd accomplished, and the obvious values alignment throughout the company. Innovation, Integrity, and Impact had taken on a life of their own.

Arun briefly stood again to echo Lynn's comments on the impact of the company's bullying and harassment initiatives. "As you know, I got some very negative feedback last year about my own impact. I had no idea others saw me as a bully, and I've been working on that. I am pleased to say that a recent 360 leadership feedback survey indicated that team members feel I have made a positive turnaround in my behavior. Two program leads even say that I have now become someone they actually choose to work with. I am grateful to you all for your support in making those changes." Everyone appeared touched by Arun's unexpected vulnerability.

Donna and Edgar now stood up together and projected on the screen a colorful image with the words "Find Something to Do Besides Bullying." Edgar showed a short video of the high school students from his son Josh's school. Several students spoke of getting help, both as bullies and as victims. One teen said she believed the program had saved her life. Donna closed by making the announcement that three other schools had reached out requesting that Tech Environments partner with them in the coming year to create similar programs. "I'd say we are seen as a very positive force for our community," Donna concluded.

Ted arose from his seat and amused everyone by pulling a large green foam dollar sign from his briefcase. "All the changes you described have cost us money," he stated. "At the same time, revenues generated this year have gone up significantly as well. We are on track this fiscal year to have our best financial performance ever. That's a tribute to everyone's hard work, and to the fact that we recognized the factors of VUCA. We responded with a strategy shaped around our values, internal and external community (aka "us"), curiosity and continuous learning, and aspiration to stay focused on our goals and to continue to grow. Our VUCA Tools approach is powerful and sustainable. The numbers support that." Ted held his foam prop aloft as he sat down.

Jack was the last to take the floor. "I am astonished and overwhelmed by the many accomplishments you all have underscored. I want to let you know that Tech Environments was chosen as a finalist this year for the Prism Award for our development of a coaching culture, and that we have been included in the Best Workplaces for Working Parents list in *Fortune's* annual publication. Those are accolades to be proud of. However, I am most gratified by how we've come together as a team. In holding each other accountable for performance and for being role models, we've become the kind of leaders I want others to emulate." Holding up his glass, Jack toasted the team. They continued to toast one another, and to enjoy a well-deserved celebration.

40

IT TAKES ALL OF US

Jack, Donna, Patrick, Edgar, Lynn, and Ted all sat on the stage, ready to launch the annual all-hands meeting, except for the fact that Arun had yet to arrive and take his seat with the rest of the senior leadership team up front. Seeing that no one seemed to know what was keeping Arun, Jack tapped the mic to make sure it was working before addressing the capacity crowd of employees.

"So," Jack boomed. "How did we do it? How did we manage to turn things around this last year and re-create Tech Environments?" Jack always opened the annual session with a statement of his vision and goals for the coming year. Twelve months earlier, Jack had been the one calling the shots for the company. He held the authority, and employees hoped the CEO would lead them out of a significant dip in their revenues and reputation. It was unusual for Jack to change his routine and to ask a question of the crowd. For many in attendance, it was further evidence of the pleasant change that had taken place in Jack's leadership. He now readily shared power, including empowering those present to come up with the answer to his question now, and to create shared understanding at this annual meeting. "Well?" Jack asked again. "How did we bring Tech Environments back from the brink of disaster, and how did we make that change sustainable?"

No one needed further encouragement, as hands flew up around the room. *Will this be a free-for-all, or the celebration of an incredible journey?* Jack wondered, still a little uncertain in his new style of leading. Holding the microphone out to a man in the front row, he watched and waited.

"What turned us around was our new values-based focus," Pete from the finance team offered. "Integrity, Innovation, and Impact. Once we established shared values we were all committed to, we began to act differently. We started to feel differently. We treated each other with respect. Having leaders who were willing to earn our trust was key."

"I liked Double-Clicking!" Raj offered next. "That helped us clarify misunderstandings between our teammates and with our clients. Our brains got in sync with one another."[20]

Another person spoke up, "I think it was the whole Victim-Creator thing, The Empowerment Dynamic. Having the 3 Vital Questions helped us stop complaining and blaming.[21] Once we started asking for what we wanted, and seeing mistakes and missteps as learning opportunities, we all took ownership for what happened. We never looked back. It's not like all the drama's gone, but we aren't addicted to drama anymore."

Several microphones were now being passed around the crowd to those with hands raised. A woman near the back of the auditorium volunteered next. "I think the critical event was us going to train with the equine coach and the horses. We saw that leaders can't force teamwork or forward movement. It has to be a partnership. It's an 'us.' The horses taught us that." She passed the mic to the person behind her.

"I think it was the Both/And!" this woman offered. "We recognized that we could both be right when we disagreed, and we started to look for ways to listen and learn instead of trying to win. It was definitely Polarity Thinking and mapping,[22] Jack. That has my vote!"

A male voice now filled the room, asserting, "I think the reversal happened because we stopped letting Arun get away with being a bully! No more bullies allowed at Tech Environments!" Everyone looked around to see who'd spoken. Then the giggling started when they realized it was Arun himself, who continued, "And in the process, we all realized Arun is really a super nice guy." The group laughed harder, before breaking into applause. Arun passed the mic to Kim, and went to take his seat with the rest of the senior leadership team at the front.

"Yes, the workplace bullying initiative was important for sure!" Kim declared. "And even better was taking it to the schools so our kids and community could benefit too." She smiled, and seeing no other hands up, tossed the mic to CFO Ted on the stage.

"I was sure the anti-bullying initiative for our schools would be too expensive, both in terms of time lost and financial cost," Ted admitted. "But it turned out that volunteering didn't reduce our productivity. Instead, it enhanced our output, engagement, teamwork, and retention. Partnering with the community to make our schools better has had more value than I can begin to quantify." Ted handed the microphone to Edgar.

"As you know, the work we've done to address the bullying problem is near and dear to my heart," Edgar addressed the crowd. "When I came back after a couple of years away, I was so curious to see if Tech Environments was the company I thought it could be. I had a million questions about what was important to you, what you really wanted. And you all shared your aspirations for who we could be. That's what made the difference. In my view, focusing on that vision is what enabled the turnaround." Seeing Lynn smiling, Edgar handed her the mic.

"I agree with so much of what many of you are saying. We've succeeded because we stopped being hung up on cost and risk. We focused on safety and sustainability," Lynn said. "When I stopped acting like a policeman, no one needed policing. We trusted each person's intention and fully committed to earning one another's respect." She handed the microphone back to Tech Environments' CEO.

Jack gestured around the room at everyone now. "You're all right. All those things, and more, transformed us. You each made a difference, and you are continuing to make one. Anyone want to sum it up? Donna, will you put your branding spin on it?"

Donna stood up and looked around her before accepting the mic from Jack. "VUCA Tools!" Her amplified voice carried easily throughout the large auditorium. "Whatever we did, we realized it all came down to four commitments: Values. Us. Curiosity. Aspirations. Every solution you all mentioned had at least one of those components, sometimes all of them. VUCA Tools for a VUCA world. That's how we did it, and how Tech Environments will keep succeeding."

And with the responding cheer that followed, Patrick released the pods of confetti positioned above the room and Tech Environments' team members were quickly covered with the small bits of flying paper.

PART 3

NOTES AND RESOURCES
FOR A DEEPER DIVE

41

VUCA TOOLS™:

ACCESSING VALUES, US, CURIOSITY, AND ASPIRATIONS FOR POWERFUL IMPACT

Volatility, Uncertainty, Complexity, and Ambiguity, aka VUCA, have created challenges for all of us as leaders, team members, and as human beings. How do we rise to these challenges?

VUCA Tools for a VUCA World offers four powerful possibilities as compelling, and complementary, solutions: Values, Us, Curiosity, and Aspirations. Throughout the book, the leaders at Tech Environments demonstrate how one or more of these tools enable effective forward movement and results. These leaders' goal, and the desire of many leaders, is sustainable success. Each of the four VUCA Tools approaches support this intention in the face of VUCA.[23]

How do the four VUCA Tools of Values, Us, Curiosity, and Aspirations help address the problems created by VUCA? This happens in many different ways, depending on both the aspect of VUCA at play (volatility, uncertainty, complexity, or ambiguity) and the individual leaders' preferences and skillsets.

Volatility: When experiencing the volatility of a challenging relationship with one another, Donna and Lynn use the **Us** VUCA Tool when they decide to tackle it together. At the same time, they employ the VUCA Tool of **Aspirations**—identifying that they'd like to strive for a more effective, better relationship instead of undermining one another and focusing on the problems in their relationship. Using The Empowerment Dynamic (TED*) provides a structure for shifting from the problem of volatility in their relationship to the aspiration of partnership.

Uncertainty and Ambiguity: The ambiguity and uncertainty of VUCA create a desire for clarity and control in many of us. One tool for gaining clarity and control is curiosity. **Curiosity** as a tool is embodied throughout many of these chapters, when leaders use open-ended questions in the peer coaching process and when Polarity Thinking, Double-Clicking, or another tool gets introduced to the team as an approach to explore diverse perspectives and the unfamiliar notion that "We could both be right."

Complexity: The world faced by the leaders in *VUCA Tools*, and by all of us, has become more complex. Companies must pay attention to their products and services, of course, and increasingly to their brand and reputation in myriad contexts. Companies must respond to what their customers and the mainstream press say, and also to social media, viral information and misinformation, and online posts to career and other search sites. Two of the challenges depicted in *VUCA Tools* are (1) negative comments on Glassdoor.com about the culture at Tech Environments and (2) an assertion in an industry article suggesting that Tech Environments is on the decline. The volume of input and feedback adds complexity to the company's tasks, requiring them to focus simultaneously on maintaining, innovating, and improving their products, creating positive employee experiences, and attending to what's being said about the company. Once again, several VUCA Tools are useful in addressing this complexity. The tool of **Us** enables the power of many—for example, HR leader Marianne gathering a group of associates to deal with harassment allegations by creating an internal anti-bullying program. A focus on **Values** enables CEO Jack to recognize that the company values of Integrity and Impact require him to hold one of their senior leaders accountable for his negative impact when he dismisses others' feelings and needs.

These examples are just a snippet of the applications of VUCA Tools. Each of the VUCA Tools are integrated throughout the story as the leaders share their visions and hopes (Aspirations), ask themselves and one another questions (Curiosity), partner with each other in re-creating a vibrant company (Us), and center on what is most important to them in their lives and in their work (Values). In the coming pages, we'll take a closer look at what constitutes the VUCA Tools of Values, Us, Curiosity, and Aspirations so that you can better see opportunities to use them in your own life, work, and organizations.

VALUES

"Values constitute your personal 'bottom line.' They serve as guides to action. They inform the priorities you set and the decisions you make. They tell you when to say yes and when to say no."—James Kouzes and Barry Posner, *The Leadership Challenge*

"Tolerance of uncertainty is about remaining open to what your mind has to say while continuing to move in the direction of core values . . ."—Todd Kashdan, *Curious?*

Our values provide the strong foundation we need as we respond to a changing world. Whether we focus on ourselves as individuals or on our teams, companies, families, or communities, creating clarity about our values provides a consistent and sustainable way to make choices. **Values** give us our solid ground despite the ever-shifting sands of our VUCA world.

EXAMPLES OF THE USE OF **VALUES** IN *VUCA TOOLS*

In Chapter 17 of *VUCA Tools for a VUCA World,* sustainability coach Edgar leads the team at Tech Environments to identify the organization's core values by inviting them to discern the qualities they want their associates to embody, what their customers want from them, and why Tech Environments exists. For Edgar, sustainability is more likely when all voices are engaged, and he solicits everyone's input by sending a company-wide invitation. The words generated through the associates' responses are used to create a word cloud that shows three words occurring more than all the others: Integrity, Innovation, and Impact. Tech Environments' senior leadership team chooses these as their company values—the values they want to honor when making decisions and holding themselves accountable. This is one benefit of company values—clarity and a strong foundation for taking aligned action.

Individual values are equally important in providing people with a strong sense of groundedness, and yet most leaders seldom consciously reflect on their values. CEO Jack gets reconnected with his values when he realizes that he's been putting work ahead of significant family events. This is the start of Jack becoming a better leader. Even more explicit, in Chapter 20, Raj encourages Kim to reflect on her own core values as a way to deal with the sense of uncertainty she is feeling. **Values** provide a solid place to stand, and this makes them a useful tool in dealing with a VUCA world.

EXERCISES TO EXPLORE VALUES

The simplest way to reflect on values is through using a list of values and choosing the ones that are most important to you, limiting the list to a manageable number—perhaps five to ten values. This is often much more difficult than people expect, particularly when the next step is to prioritize these values from the most important to the still very important but least critical ones. See the list of values below and do this yourself:

1. Select the ten values that you consciously choose to live your life by, the values you consider when you are making decisions. If there are some values you hold as important that aren't included on the list, add them.

Acceptance	Empathy	Loyalty	Success
Accomplishment	Endurance	Obedience	Teamwork
Accuracy	Excellence	Openness	Timeliness
Achievement	Expressiveness	Optimism	Tradition
Adaptability	Fairness	Order	Tranquility
Adventure	Faith	Peace	Trust
Affection	Fame	Perfection	Uniqueness
Altruism	Family	Playfulness	Usefulness
Ambition	Fluency	Poise	Variety
Approachability	Focus	Popularity	Virtue
Attractiveness	Frankness	Power	Vision
Balance	Freedom	Resourcefulness	Warmth
Beauty	Friendliness	Respect	Wealth
Calmness	Fun	Rigor	Winning
Challenge	Generosity	Security	Wisdom
Cheerfulness	Gratitude	Self-control	Wonder
Cleanliness	Hard Work	Selflessness	
Comfort	Innovation	Self-reliance	
Commitment	Integrity	Service	
Compassion	Intelligence	Sharing	
Connection	Intimacy	Significance	
Consistency	Intrepidness	Simplicity	
Contribution	Intuition	Sincerity	
Directness	Joy	Solitude	
Discipline	Justice	Speed	
Diversity	Kindness	Spirituality	
Duty	Knowledge	Spontaneity	
Economy	Learning	Stability	
Efficiency	Love	Structure	

2. Put your values in order from 1 to 10. The order matters, since our ever-changing and VUCA world ensures that all of us will experience frequent challenges, and these situations will sometimes present us with the pull of competing values.

3. Define what you mean by each value. For example, if health is on your list, you might define it as the sense of personal emotional and physical well-being, or as the "ability to function effectively, to cope adequately, to change appropriately, and to grow from within," a definition which can apply to an individual, a team, or an organization (Source: Organizational Health Diagnostic and Development Corporation). In addition to defining what each value means, identify your success criteria. How will you know you are living this value?

4. Consider challenging ways to engage with your own values, those of your team members, and those of clients you are working with:

   a. Alignment: How well do your values match the organization's espoused or apparent values? For example, in *VUCA Tools*, Kim's highest-priority value of family appears well-aligned with Tech Environments' decision to bring their anti-bullying program into the community, beginning with the high school of one of the senior leaders' sons. In contrast, if it appears that CEO Jack is willing to sacrifice key family events like his daughter's college graduation for the sake of work, Kim may begin to believe that her priority value of family is misaligned with company practices, and that it's not the right organization for her.

   b. Time management: Assess how your team is spending its time. Are the hours dedicated to each task and responsibility reflective of the values you say you hold? Look at a typical week and consider the purpose(s) of each activity. Twenty-five hours a week spent in meetings may have the espoused purposes of effective communication and teamwork. Yet, while a value of communication is being prioritized, values such as impact, efficiency, and independence may be marginalized. Awareness of values can enable different choices in how time is allotted to activities, or in structuring the activities themselves. For example, a 15-minute standing meeting each Monday morning may be used constructively to embody values including communication and efficiency. A monthly recap and team celebration focused specifically on shared accomplishments might exemplify values of teamwork and impact. Whether you are leading a team, coaching a team, or both, paying attention to the alignment between time commitments and chosen values will yield dividends.

c. Decision-making: What is a decision you need to make? What options are there that will honor most or all of your values? What decision will be made if there are others involved? Are there shared values you can agree on? What are your priority values? Leaders at Tech Environments sometimes put loyalty as a high value, and this may have led to not holding individuals accountable for behaviors because they were unwilling to challenge a leader who'd been loyal to the company.

RESOURCES

- Todd Kashdan, *Curious?* (Harper Perennial, 2010).

- Harry M. Kraemer Jr., *From Values to Action: The Four Principles of Values-Based Leadership* (Jossey-Bass, 2011).

- Meg Rentschler with Steve Sosland, "Establishing a Values Culture," StaR Coach Show, Podcast #50, http://www.starcoach-show.com/50-establishing-values-culture-steve-sosland/.

US

"I think we so often equate leadership with being experts—the leader is supposed to come in and fix things. But in this interconnected world we live in now, it's almost impossible for just one person to do that."—Jacqueline Novogratz

"Teamwork represents a set of values that encourage listening and responding constructively to views expressed by others, giving others the benefit of the doubt, providing support, and recognizing the interests and achievements of others."—Jon R. Katzenbach and Douglas K. Smith

We don't accomplish incredible things solo. No single person is an expert in everything. No individual can see the whole without help—we each see from our own unique perspective based on our values, experiences, preferences, and aspirations. The inherent limitations, as well as potential brilliance, of each human being is what makes accessing the VUCA Tool of **Us** such a critically important tool when we're faced with the challenges of VUCA.

EXAMPLES OF **US** IN *VUCA TOOLS FOR A VUCA WORLD*

In *VUCA Tools*, leaders accomplish their goals in a VUCA environment through consistently accessing one another's skillsets and inviting other perspectives. Peer coaching is built in to their leadership development, a continuation from the previous book, *Being Coached*. Each leader becomes more effective through his or her relationships and feedback from peers. Patrick relies on input from team members to develop a clearer sense that he is indeed effective in his role at Tech Environments. His choice to engage Marianne in owning a key project demonstrates the importance of **Us**—Patrick has listened to her desire to lead and is willing to delegate, recognizing that his own capacity is limited. Accessing Us is more powerful than defaulting to self-reliance. Even Patrick's willingness to consider the feedback posted on the Glassdoor.com website demonstrates the importance of **Us**—he needs this additional input to fully comprehend the detrimental impact of certain leaders' behaviors on Tech Environments' ability to recruit quality talent and retain existing team members.

It is evident throughout *VUCA Tools* that much of the company's reinventing itself happens through the **Us** of team members communicating and working together. The leaders do a polarity map together to learn about the benefits of both stability and innovation to enable themselves to consciously access both instead of lurching between the two. In another example, Lynn and Donna struggle with their different styles and perspectives before taking the time to forge a shared understanding through The Empowerment Dynamic approach. Each alone is a powerful leader, and they waste energy and time when they choose to be adversarial. Together they become infinitely more powerful in moving in the direction of their individual visions and their shared goals.

Us can be two people, a team, or an organization. It can also go beyond the organization. In Chapter 35, "Sometimes the 'Us' Is a Horse," they address the need for perspective shifts and new experiences in equine coaching to see themselves clearly. Another example of **Us** outside the organization is the leaders' leveraging the feedback of a negative industry magazine review to take a deep look at the changing needs and expectations of their clients. The volatility of their environment means that accessing Us, in whatever form it takes, will enable a more agile and effective response to VUCA.

WAYS TO PRACTICE US

1. Ask "Who sees this differently? What can I learn from them?" Before asserting your own viewpoint, commit to understanding theirs fully. This approach yields dividends whether it's a customer, your child or significant other, or workplace colleagues.

2. Notice situations of conflict or where you keep solving the same problem repeatedly. Identify the polarity pair (conflicting values, strategies, or perspectives) at play and map the upsides and downsides of both poles. Read Barry Johnson's books and visit www. PolarityPartnerships.com to learn more.

3. Buy a deck of collaboration cards such as We! Connect cards (https:// weand.me/store/) or Michael Michalko's ThinkPak brainstorming tool (http://creativethinking.net). Pick a card at the start of a project meeting, or whenever you want to remind yourself of the value of Us.

4. Express appreciation to another person, both for who they are as a person and for their positive impact. *The Five Languages of Appreciation in the Workplace* offers insight about how to match your style of appreciation to the language the other person most prefers.

5. Make the shift from drama to empowerment through asking the "3 Vital Questions® for Work and Life."

RESOURCES

- Amy Gallo, "Why We Should Be Disagreeing More at Work," *Harvard Business Review*, Jan. 3, 2018, https://hbr.org/2018/01/ why-we-should-be-disagreeing-more-at-work.

- Judith E. Glaser, *Conversational Intelligence: How Great Leaders Build Trust and Get Extraordinary Results* (Routledge, 2016).

- Theresa Johnston, "Mark Leslie: Putting the 'We' in Leadership," Stanford Business Insights, October 6, 2015, https://www.gsb. stanford.edu/insights/mark-leslie-putting-we-leadership.

- David Emerald Womeldorff and Donna Zajonc, "3 Vital Questions® for Work & Life: A strategic approach to creating engaged, innovative, and resilient workplaces by applying *The Power of TED* (*The Empowerment Dynamic)*." (https://elearning.powerofted.com/ Use coupon code adeat$50 to receive a $50 discount on the online course)

CURIOSITY

"Most people overestimate risk, failure, and danger and underestimate the value of being curious."—Todd Kashdan

"As our workplaces, homes, and communities become more diverse, conflicting values are inevitable, but our negative reactions to conflict are not! The solution to conflict is not to avoid it, but to recognize it and respond with curiosity to defuse negative emotions early on."—Kathy Taberner and Kirsten Taberner Siggins

VUCA is challenging because we aren't sure what to expect. We don't know, and that's uncomfortable. One of the best ways to deal with not knowing is to ask questions, to dive in and discover. **Curiosity** opens doors and knocks down barriers. With curiosity, we enlarge what we know (or think we know) and explore what could be. We expand perspective, and this helps us build on the Us of VUCA Tools as we recognize that more than one person can have the answer, that our joint perspectives frequently provide a more complete picture. **Curiosity** is empowering; it gives us a crucial skill for responding to VUCA.

HOW **CURIOSITY** SHOWS UP IN
VUCA TOOLS FOR A VUCA WORLD

In *VUCA Tools for a VUCA World*, **Curiosity** is embedded in the culture of Tech Environments. Years earlier (see *Being Coached*), the Tech

Environments' team embraced peer coaching and team coaching. These leaders know a great deal about generating answers by asking good questions. Beginning with Ted's asking his team what they should be talking about in Chapter 4, and continuing with Arun's peer coaching of Patrick in the following chapter, the leaders at Tech Environments are consistently coping with our VUCA world through asking curious questions.

Another approach to **Curiosity** in *VUCA Tools* is our glimpses into the leaders' reflections on themselves. Tech Environments' leaders are not just asking one another questions; they are also taking time to reflect and asking themselves curious questions. When doing so in a manner that is not self-critical, this kind of curiosity has significant positive impact. Jordan's coaching sessions with individual leaders underscore the importance of curiosity and open-ended questions in enabling each leader to discover his or her own answers.

In addition to the kinds of questions and coaching approach noted above, *VUCA Tools* also depicts a culture that supports curiosity through sharing tools and concepts, and by offering stretch assignments to develop leaders. Patrick's introduction of Double-Clicking at a Lunch & Learn in Chapter 19 provides support for curiosity, exploring what is behind words instead of assuming we know. Offering Marianne an opportunity to lead the internal anti-bullying initiative supports her curiosity, and also buttresses Patrick's curiosity and learning as he sees her approach this task differently than he would.

EXERCISES TO USE AND ENHANCE CURIOSITY

1. Be present. Choose your focus and set aside and say "no" to distractions. Kathy Taberner and Kirsten Taberner Siggins offer the ABSORB process for how to be fully present in their book *The Power of Curiosity: How To Have Real Conversations That Create Collaboration, Innovation and Understanding*. Many mindfulness practices will also strengthen your awareness of how to be present and your capacity for curiosity.

2. Double-Click instead of assuming you understand what a word means or what another person is saying. (Judith E. Glaser, *Conversational Intelligence*)

3. Ask open-ended, non-leading questions with an intention to learn and discover. Several of the references below, including both books noted in 1 and 2 above, offer suggestions for improving the quality of the questions you ask.

4. Do experiments involving situations, people, and strategies you are curious about. Your experiments can be as simple as trying to eliminate the word "but" from your vocabulary to enable you to be more open to differing points of view.

5. If you are striving to create a culture of curiosity in your organization, Katie Smith Milway and Alex Goldmark suggest these four ways to grow curiosity in your workplace culture: Encourage inquiry. Write agendas as questions. Avoid blame. Assume all learning is good. Consider trying one or all of them.

RESOURCES

- Warren Berger, *A More Beautiful Question: The Power of Inquiry to Spark Breakthrough Ideas* (Bloomsbury USA, 2014).

- Judith E. Glaser, *Conversational Intelligence: How Great Leaders Build Trust and Get Extraordinary Results* (Routledge, 2016).

- Todd Kashdan, *Curious?* (Harper Perennial, 2010).

- Katie Smith Milway and Alex Goldmark, "Four Ways to Create a Culture of Curiosity," *Harvard Business Review*, September 18, 2013, https://hbr.org/2013/09/four-ways-to-cultivate-a-culture-of-curiosity.

- Kathy Taberner and Kirsten Taberner Siggins, *The Power of Curiosity: How To Have Real Conversations That Create Collaboration, Innovation and Understanding* (Morgan James Publishing, 2015).

ASPIRATIONS

"Being forward-looking—envisioning exciting possibilities and enlisting others in a shared view of the future—is the attribute that most distinguishes leaders from nonleaders."—James Kouzes and Barry Posner

"If one advances confidently in the direction of his dreams, and endeavors to live the life which he has imagined, he will meet with a success unexpected in common hours."—Henry David Thoreau

What do I want? What do we want? These are our aspirations. Aspirations provide the vision, the energy, and the clarity that enable us to move forward. Rather than staying immersed in the problems of VUCA, Aspirations are an invitation to consider attending instead to what you are hoping to create. Doing so may cause trepidation. Yet aspirations also provide drive, enable you to access your brain's best thinking, and offer inspiration to others.

HOW **ASPIRATIONS** SHOW UP IN *VUCA TOOLS*

In *VUCA Tools*, Donna is the first one to challenge the leadership team to emphasize **Aspirations** when she asks the SLT to identify what "thriving" looks like for Tech Environments rather than concentrating their energy on merely surviving the perceived threats of VUCA. Donna's suggestion helps shift the team from fearing their VUCA environment to determination to realize their vision for the company. In her interactions with Lynn too, Donna makes the shift from seeing her colleague as a problem to understanding that it is up to the two of them to engage with each other in a consciously positive way. *The Empowerment Dynamic (TED*)* offers a structure and shared language for the pair to transform their relationship, later inspiring other women leaders by sharing their story.

In a similarly inspiring vein, Edgar's aspiration of creating sustainable cultures enables him to take the risk of not being paid for his work because he has such a clear vision of how he can help. In aspiring to share the gifts and wisdom he has acquired, Edgar's confidence and optimism are contagious, energizing the Tech Environments' leadership team at one of their lowest points.

Also aspirational is the way Tech Environments elects to respond to concerns about bullying and harassment, both in their own company and in community schools. They take action to create collaborative programs to help bullies and all those impacted by them to "find something better to do." In doing so, they discover and leverage their power in service of creating more positive cultures that enhance each person instead of victimizing anyone.

Even the time that Jack and his team spend with the horses and the equine coach highlights the impact of **Aspirations**—this time their power to span the divide between species. Once Tech Environments' leaders become centered in themselves and clear about what they want the horse to do, they are able to partner effectively with the horse to achieve their goals.

EXERCISES TO LEVERAGE **ASPIRATIONS**

1. When you find yourself complaining, consider instead identifying what you want. In *TED** language, pinpoint the desire that is being thwarted. Then choose at least one small step to move you in the direction of your vision.

2. Embrace the Both/And of Polarity Thinking when faced with the threat of VUCA. Consciously choose to spend as much energy identifying and realizing possibility as on identifying and mitigating risk.

3. Aspiration requires dedicated thought. Commit time for reflection. During this time, set aside busyness and focus on what you aspire to do or be. You may even want to choose a visual image to capture your envisioned future. The Center for Creative Leadership's Visual Explorer cards and RealResults' InSight decks both offer compelling and evocative pictures to capture your mind's view.

4. On your team, share your aspirations with one another. Katzenbach and Smith describe true teams as those "that encourage listening and responding constructively to views expressed by others, giving others the benefit of the doubt, providing support, and recognizing the interests and achievements of others." Aspire to be this kind of team, where each person is willing to take risks to share their deepest desires, trusting that they will be accepted and supported by others.

5. Appreciative Inquiry is an approach that supports a focus on what's right and what's possible. Explore the Appreciative Inquiry Commons for exercises, for yourself and with your team.

RESOURCES TO ENABLE YOU TO ACCESS AND EMBODY ASPIRATIONS

- Appreciative Inquiry Commons, https://appreciativeinquiry. champlain.edu/.

- CCL Visual Explorer. http://www.ccl-explorer.org/

- David Emerald, *The Power of TED*: The Empowerment Dynamic* (Smashwords, 2016).

- RealResults InSights cards. https://squareup.com/market/ real-results-coach-training/item/insights-cards

- James M. Kouzes and Barry Posner, "To Lead, Create a Shared Vision," *Harvard Business Review*, January 2009, https://hbr.org/2009/01/to-lead-create-a-shared-vision.

42

THE VALUE OF STORYTELLING IN LEADING AND LEARNING

"Story doesn't grab power. Story creates power. You do not need a position of formal leadership when you know the power of story. Like the sword of Excalibur, story conjures a magical power that does not need formal authority to work. It creates another kind of status and power all its own. As a storyteller you borrow a story's power to connect people to what is important and to help them make sense of their world." (Annette Simmons, *The Story Factor*, p. 15)

Many readers will question why most of this book is a story rather than a didactic description of VUCA and how to use VUCA Tools™. There are many reasons I've chosen to tell a story, the most significant one being that stories are both enjoyable and memorable. We tend to like stories and therefore persist in reading (or listening to) them.

Stories offer connection, an easy framework for our minds when it comes to retrieving important tools and concepts. Now that you know Jack and Lynn and Arun and the others in this book, you'll find that the VUCA Tools shared are relevant to you in part because they made a difference to leaders who are like yourself. When you consider the cost of drama at work, Lynn and Donna may come to mind, as you remember how powerful they found *The Empowerment Dynamic (TED*)* to be in creating a more successful and congenial working relationship with one another. When you recognize lack of confidence that can get in the way of being effective, you may recall Patrick and the success of his Lunch & Learn on Double-Clicking as well as his growing confidence when he stopped assuming he was not ready for his leadership role and began taking in the positive feedback he was receiving. All these details are easier to retain and to access when they are part of a story.

Why are stories so enjoyable and memorable? There is a neuroscience behind storytelling that explains its impact, and it has to do with brain activation. Just as we might say we are engaged by stories, our brain is also engaged by them. We know this through studies of brain activity when individuals are provided with a list of neutral words versus strong sensory words or a story. The more engaged the brain is, the more places a memory gets stored. Thus, stories play a role in creating numerous access points so that valuable information and tools can later be retrieved.

ENGAGING WITH STORIES

To take a deeper dive into storytelling, consider some of the following exercises.

1. Create stories based on your own experiences of using each of the VUCA Tools shared here to deal with your own constantly changing VUCA environment. When have you found that you didn't have the knowledge or capacity to accomplish a task, only to realize that your team did—that **Us** was necessary to deal with Complexity? How have you experienced a conflict between **Values**, and used a tool such as asking questions or engaging multiple stakeholders' per-

spectives to forge a path of shared values that enabled forward movement? And, on the flip side, where have you failed to use VUCA Tools when you needed them? What, perhaps, is a story of where you focused on the threat of VUCA and let the volatility or the ambiguity overwhelm you instead of accessing one of the VUCA Tools and approaches shared here? Create your own powerful stories to influence your colleagues and shape your culture.

2. When you read fiction, whether it's a novel for your own enjoyment or a children's book you are reading to your child, use the opportunity to grow your familiarity with VUCA—volatility, uncertainty, complexity, and ambiguity. Notice how each of these contributes to the drama and tension of the story. Which one of the VUCA Tools does the author use to deal with this tension?

3. Start your meetings with stories. In a client meeting where there's doubt about how they'll convince users to adopt a new technology, tell a story about a success when someone took a leap of faith and embraced an innovation.

4. Stories can be valuable in almost any of the challenging situations that arise in VUCA contexts, whether it's bullying or a loss of relevance or the need for a new perspective or skillset. Create or find the stories that will energize you and your organization.

The resources shared below will offer more structure and clarity about how to develop, tell, and leverage stories to create the sustainable success and culture you desire.

RESOURCES

- Lisa Bloom, The Story Coach, www.story-coach.com.

- Stephen Denning, *The Leader's Guide to Storytelling* (John Wiley and Sons, 2005).

- Peter Schroeder, "The Neuroscience of Storytelling Will Make You Rethink the Way You Create," eLearning Industry, September 19, 2017, https://elearningindustry.com/neuroscience-of-storytelling-will-make-rethink-way-create

- Annette Simmons, *The Story Factor* (Basic Books, 2006).

43

COACHING OPTIONS FOR EFFECTIVE LEADERS AND TEAMS

At the heart of *VUCA Tools for a VUCA World* is teamwork, a group of senior leaders working together to enable their organization to cope with the challenges posed by volatility, uncertainty, complexity, and ambiguity. Equally at the heart of VUCA Tools is coaching, a crucial tool for enabling individuals and teams to learn and grow. Coaching is critical throughout the book in helping these leaders move from where they are to where they long to be. The various coaching relationships and situations shared throughout the book depict the supportive and challenging coaching interactions that can enable self-discovery and awareness, the first steps on the path to change.

PEER COACHING

"If we can coach individuals to come up with their own solutions that they are committed to, this will ultimately be far more effective than a 'better' solution we offer that they are less committed to." (John Zenger and Kathleen Stinnett, *The Extraordinary Coach*, p. 15)

When you meet the Tech Environments' team in *VUCA Tools*, they already have a history with coaching. You may have read about their adventures several years earlier in *Being Coached: Group and Team Coaching from the Inside*. At that time the team engaged with Coach Jordan to help their middle managers, and then their senior leadership team, to become more effective as leaders. This experience provided Tech Environments' team members with key skills in peer coaching. In *VUCA Tools*, the leaders have continued to incorporate peer coaching in their team interactions, both spontaneously and as a regular occurrence.

VUCA Tools Chapter 5, "It's Not About You," depicts Arun coaching Patrick through a crisis of confidence in his leadership effectiveness. In the process of eavesdropping on their coaching, we the readers are reminded of the importance of a nonjudgmental attitude, confidentiality, deep listening, open-ended questions, and the peer coach choosing to enable the other to access their own wisdom rather than giving advice. Moreover, Arun's coaching offers a structure of accountability to Patrick for following through on taking action. For readers who want to develop their own peer coaching skills, *The Extraordinary Coach* and *The Coaching Habit*, among other wonderful books and programs, provide guidance.

LEADERSHIP COACHING

"The promise of coaching is not so much that it provides instant solutions, but rather that it promotes learning and change over time." (De Haan, Culpin, and Curd, 2011)

"The essence of executive coaching is helping leaders work through challenges so they can transform their learning into results for the organization." (Mary Beth O'Neill, *Executive Coaching with Backbone and Heart*)

Peer coaching can often be effective at eliciting another's wisdom. Yet coaching by peers is not always enough. There are several reasons that a professional coach may be needed. First, a professional coach has typically had more training and dedicated coaching experience than most peer coaches. Second, professional coaches recognize that many of the benefits of coaching are realized when the client, or coachee, comes to the coaching conversation with their own agenda, and the coach honors that agenda rather than bringing his/her own goals for the session. This commitment to the coachee's agenda is powerful—it's all about them. Yet, it can be challenging when a coach and coachee are peers in an organization, have varied hats to wear, and at times even have competing agendas.

Enter the external coach. In this case, Coach Jordan has a long-standing relationship with Tech Environments. She has the benefit of knowing the organization and its leaders while also having the advantage of objectivity. Tech Environments' leaders engage her coaching services at several points in *VUCA Tools*. Arun is particularly appreciative of having Jordan available at points of high stress. In Chapter 12, Arun reaches out to Jordan when he recognizes that he may need to up his game and that of his department. Tech Environments has been highlighted as a company on the decline in its innovativeness, and Arun holds himself accountable for this. Added to the stress is his concern that CEO Jack also holds him accountable. Coaching provides an avenue for Arun to surface his thoughts and feelings, including the conclusion he's come to that wearing two hats on the senior leadership team is not sustainable. Though this session doesn't resolve his challenges, it enables Arun to identify a next step for moving forward.

Patrick and Arun each reach out to Jordan again later in the book to deal with challenges. In each case, the individual coaching sessions offer a mix of support and challenge. Jordan's acceptance and support enables her coachees to show vulnerability and take risks in voicing their fears.

Her challenging stance communicates her belief that each of these leaders is up to the task. When coaching Patrick in Chapter 26, for example, Jordan challenges his high expectations of himself with a touch of humor when she comments, "If I'm not mistaken, you just described Superman. You were just getting to the part about how you ought to be able to read people's minds with your x-ray vision." In Chapter 28, Jordan's challenge to Arun pushes him to consider the question "What happens if nothing changes?" and to recognize that his current state is not sustainable. For both of these clients, clarity and momentum are created in the coaching sessions, and Arun and Patrick leave her office with greater awareness as well as the sense that they are not alone on their journeys.

TEAM COACHING

"Team coaching is educational; the ultimate aim is to help the team develop the capacity to coach itself."—Paul Lawrence and Ann Whyte, "What do experienced team coaches do?" *International Journal of Evidence Based Coaching and Mentoring* 15(1), February 2017

Groups and teams are not the same. Teams have a common goal or goals, and are judged at least in part by their collective performance. Each person on a team is interdependent with the others, expected to be accountable for not only their own performance but also for enabling the success of others on the team. At Tech Environments, the senior leadership team is struggling when we meet them at the start of *VUCA Tools*. Rather than benefiting from their different styles and perspectives, their differences are the source of conflict. They are finding fault with one another. With the increased pressure from VUCA, each leader seems to be responding by narrowing his or her focus, resulting in silos instead of a collaborative team.

Team coaching offers Tech Environments' SLT the opportunity to reestablish a set of common goals, to recommit to their shared organizational values, and to renew their awareness that working as a team is essential to their effectiveness. Edgar, a former member of the leadership team, comes back to Tech Environments to play the role of sustainability coach. In this role, he helps the team to reconstruct their foundation for working together. Once Edgar has rejoined the team as an ongoing member, Jordan steps in to coach them, inviting in consultant Barry for his expertise in helping team members bridge their differences through Polarity Thinking and mapping. Jordan's use of an external consultant enables her to stay in more of a coaching role while letting Barry play the role of expert. Again, we see how valuable it is to have an external coach who knows the organization and its leaders well, and yet has greater objectivity and access to diverse approaches because she is external.

EQUINE COACHING

"A horse will never willingly follow a doubtful, scattered, or passive leader. If you are calm, sincere, and clear, the horse will usually follow your lead. . . . And, if you request one thing, but believe something different in your heart, the horse will reflect this incongruence, and be confused and unable to process the request." (Shari Jaeger Goodwin, *Take the Reins: 7 Secrets to Inspired Leadership*, p. 20)

"The combination of the human educator (coach, therapist) and the equine guide offers unique, powerful, experiential exercises geared towards developing self-knowledge and self-responsibility." (Ariana Strozzi, *Horse Sense for the Leader Within*, Amazon Digital Services, 2013. Kindle)

While equine coaching is unfamiliar to most leaders and organizations, there is increasing recognition that horses can be uniquely powerful in creating an experience of ourselves that offers surprising clarity and enduring wisdom. In Chapter 14 of *VUCA Tools*, CEO Jack follows

Coach Jordan's recommendation and has an experience of equine coaching. In the process, Jack realizes that, when he feels pressure to perform, he tries to direct and coerce rather than partner with others. He quickly recognizes that the horse is not impressed by his CEO title, and that she outweighs him by a thousand pounds. There must be another way, and Jack discovers that indeed there is: he has to relearn to listen to what others need rather than only seeing things through his own perspective. Jack wisely takes this awareness and begins to apply it to bring himself and his organization back into alignment with what is most important.

Jack is so taken with his own experience of equine coaching that he decides to invest in his team as well. In the group's experience with the horse in Chapter 35, team members Lynn and Pete and Arun experience the role of trust and mutual respect for one another. Learning to connect again with each other enables them to lead the horse in an integrated and effective fashion. Clearly silos have no place in a horse pen when a horse is looking for consistent leadership. Is it possible that they aren't the most effective way to lead at Tech Environments either? In the weeks that follow, Jack is impressed with the impact of the equine coaching experience on them as individual leaders and as a team.

There are now numerous books on leadership coaching using horses, as well as training programs for equine coaches. I've been a "coach on the side" in several equine coaching engagements and can attest to the impact for individual leaders, and the power of the "aha!" experience when a team recognizes that their inability to coordinate action in the ring with a horse has an equally negative impact with their team in the organization.

Obviously, there is much more that could be shared about coaching and its wide array of unique approaches. My hope is that experiencing coaching through the eyes of Tech Environments' leaders will spark your interest to continue to explore and develop your own coaching knowledge and to experience the power of coaching for yourself.

RESOURCES

- Ann V. Deaton and Holly Williams, *Being Coached: Group and Team Coaching from the Inside* (Magus Group, 2014).
- Erik de Haan, Vicki Culpin, and Judy Curd, "Executive Coaching in Practice: What Determines Helpfulness for Clients of Coaching?" *Personnel Review* 40(1) (2011): 24–44.
- Gay Gaddis, "4 Surprising Leadership Lessons This CEO Learned from Her Horse," *Fortune*, July 19, 2015, http://fortune.com/2015/07/19/gay-gaddis-leading-during-change/.
- Shari Jaeger Goodwin, *Take the Reins! 7 Secrets to Inspired Leadership* (Kozik Rocha, 2013).
- Search https://coachfederation.org/find-a-coach to find a coach with the expertise and experience you need.
- Paul Lawrence and Ann Whyte, "What Do Experienced Team Coaches Do?" *International Journal of Evidence Based Coaching and Mentoring* 15(1), February 2017.
- Michael Bungay Stanier, *The Coaching Habit* (Box of Crayons Press, 2016).
- Ariana Strozzi, *Horse Sense for the Leader Within* (Amazon Digital Services, 2013. Kindle).
- John Zenger and Katherine Stinnett, *The Extraordinary Coach* (McGraw-Hill, 2010).

44

NEUROSCIENCE AND VUCA

"You can damage [your brain], especially if you choose to focus on something that makes you frightened or angry. ... 'rumination' ... is clearly hazardous to your health. In a Stanford brain scan study, people who focused on negative aspects of themselves, or a negative interpretation of life, had increased activity in their amygdala. This generated waves of fear, releasing a torrent of destructive neurochemicals into the brain."—Newberg and Waldman

"Curiosity is hard-wired in the brain, and its specific function is to urge us to explore, discover, and grow. It is the engine of our evolving self."—Todd Kashdan, *Curious?*

My first career was as a clinical psychologist specializing in health psychology and neuropsychology. Early in my training, one of the basic tenets we learned was that the adult brain is fully developed and static, that our brains don't keep changing once we reach a certain age. Fast-forward a few decades and we know that this clear principle was not just misguided but wrong. Our brains are changing all the time in response to our learning, our experiences, our relationships, our behavior, and our environment. So not only is the neuroscience changing all the time, but our brains are doing so as well. The volume of change obviously makes it challenging to capture here some critical neuroscience discoveries that impact leadership and teams, and yet I would feel remiss if I failed to highlight such a valuable area of knowledge.

Neuroscience is the study of how the brain and nervous system functions. Our human persistence and curiosity, coupled with technology that enables dynamic brain scanning, imaging, and mapping have dramatically expanded our understanding of how our neurology manifests in how we think, feel, and act. The past several decades has seen an explosion in our knowledge about how the brain processes and interprets our environment (the inputs), and how those interpretations are reflected in our actions. In *VUCA Tools*, Raj is the resident neuroscience expert, having become intrigued by the neuroscience of leadership in our earlier book *Being Coached*. Raj is regularly consulted by several of Tech Environments' other leaders as they tap into his wisdom to make sense of themselves as leaders—who they are at their best, and who they are when experiencing insecurity and distrust.

A review of neuroscience goes well beyond the scope of this book, particularly since the science is changing on nearly a daily basis (talk about VUCA!). Like Raj, however, many readers will want to explore more deeply the science behind how our human brains enable, and limit, our capacity to respond to VUCA. A few of the discoveries you may want to explore include the following:

- The impact of feeling safe and cared for on cognitive function
- Threat and survival response—neurochemical, and brain activation
- Our limited ability to process disconfirming information
- How negative thinking (rumination) and positivity affect our brains
- Limbic resonance—our connected brains
- How emotion contributes to decision-making

- Why visualization of success works so well
- How habits increase efficiency, and how to rewire our brains
- Self-care behaviors that enhance brain function

Here's hoping your own VUCA Tool of Curiosity enables you to explore these and many more, and use what you learn to make powerful changes in your leadership and your team.

RESOURCES

- Judith E. Glaser, "Your Brain Is Hooked on Being Right," *HBR*, Feb. 28, 2013, https://hbr.org/2013/02/break-your-addiction-to-being.
- Daniel Goleman, *Emotional Intelligence: Why It Can Matter More Than IQ* (Bantam Books, 1995).
- Jonas T. Kaplan, Sarah I. Gimbel, and Sam Harris, "Neural Correlates of Maintaining One's Political Beliefs in the Face of Counterevidence," *Scientific Reports*, December 2016, DOI: 10.1038/srep39589.
- Jan Jones-Schenk, "Foundations of Well-Being," *The Journal of Continuing Education in Nursing*, June 2017, https://doi.org/10.3928/00220124-20170517-03
- Andrew Newberg and Mark Robert Waldman, *How God Changes Your Brain* (Ballantine Books, 2010), 39.
- David Rock, *Quiet Leadership* (HarperBusiness, 2009).
- Adam Waytz and Malia Mason, "Your Brain at Work: What a New Approach to Neuroscience Can Teach Us about Management," *HBR*, July–Aug 2013, https://hbr.org/2013/07/your-brain-at-work.
- Paul J. Zak, "The Neuroscience of Trust," *HBR*, Jan-Feb. 2017.

ABOUT THE AUTHOR

After her first career in health care, Ann earned her leadership coaching certification from the Newfield Network in 2003. She founded DaVinci Resources to focus on coaching in health care in 2003 and joined The Bounce Collective leadership development in 2009. In her coaching in corporate, health care, government, and not-for-profit organizations, Ann works with leaders and teams experiencing significant change and challenge. Her favorite approaches include many of those highlighted in this book, including Polarity Thinking, Conversational Intelligence, and The Empowerment Dynamic. Ann also loves using visual imagery in her work with clients, as well as assessments that grow their self-awareness. The Change Style Indicator tool is especially useful in understanding the gifts of individuals and teams as they respond to VUCA. Ann's strengths are in creating the kinds of rich and open conversations that expand perspectives and ideas—and then supporting her clients to take action and realize their goals.

Ann earned her doctorate in Clinical Psychology from The University of Texas at Austin, with specializations in health psychology and neuropsychology. She has always appreciated the power of teams, both as a psychologist doing group therapy early in her career and for the past 15 years as a coach working with groups and teams. In addition to coaching, Ann enjoys having a ripple effect in the world through mentoring other coaches, and facilitating experiential workshops at organizations, conferences, and the Center for Corporate Education at Virginia Commonwealth University. Ann is co-author, with Holly Williams, of the book *Being Coached: Group and Team Coaching from the Inside.*

When she's not working, Ann loves to travel and experience the unique aspects of diverse people, places, and cultures. She lives with her family in Richmond, Virginia, where they've recently increased the VUCA in their own lives with the addition of an Australian Shepherd puppy. He reminds us every day of what's important—love, laughter, and learning. You can reach Ann at ann@wecanbounce.com.

INTERVIEW WITH MEG RENTSCHLER

Edited transcript excerpt from STaR Coach podcast interview with Meg Rentschler

Meg: Ann, I want to welcome you back to the STaR Coach Show. Thanks for coming back and sharing your new book with us today.

Ann: Thanks so much, Meg. Of course I'm delighted to talk with you again, and really excited to share my book *VUCA Tools for a VUCA World* as well.

Meg: In talking about such an important issue—the whole concept of VUCA—the piece that stood out for me is the concept of not just that there's this volatility that can occur, but that you want companies to be able to thrive in the face of a changing terrain. There is so much changing terrain that I love that you wrote this book to bring perspective to how can we thrive, not just survive.

Why don't we start with talking about this concept of VUCA, and how we pay attention to things that can affect an entire business, the teams within a business, and each one of us as we try to lead in the face of change. What is VUCA and how can it impact companies?

Ann: Really good question, Meg. VUCA is a term that actually came out of the Army War College in the early 1990s. It arose because the way in which we were approaching war didn't work anymore; things had changed. You couldn't use the same predictable approaches and strategies. The V in VUCA stands for Volatility, the up-and-down rollercoaster of change. U is for Uncertainty— things aren't predictable anymore; we don't have certainty that if I do this, that will happen. The C is Complexity, the sheer volume of data, of stakeholders, of information. And then A is Ambiguity, that amorphous "What am I dealing with?"

That's where VUCA came from. And for a long time, I would say VUCA wasn't known in the business world. I didn't hear about it until maybe ten years ago, and then I started hearing companies talking about VUCA, and seeing articles in *HBR*. So VUCA has really now made the transition into businesses and nonprofit organizations. A lot of different organizations I work with will say, "It's such a VUCA world now." Usually they are talking about their sense of threat and not having a handle on how to do business in this VUCA world.

Meg: Just thinking about those four elements, how uncertain they make us feel, and just how vulnerable and unsafe. Ambiguity— people don't want ambiguity. They want to know what's going to happen next. What I notice in the book that you've written, and that I had the honor to read, is how vulnerability can make us sort of turn against one another. I think we see that as we coach in organizations when there are uncertainties. A lot of finger-pointing starts to happen.

So you created a different acronym for VUCA, and sort of the antidote for VUCA, in your book, the tools we might need.

Can you tell us a little bit about the sort of tools that we might think about when we're working in this VUCA environment?

Ann: I love you saying "VUCA" in a spooky kind of way, Meg. Yes, it kept coming up for me that when we are focused on the threat and the problem, and focused on our vulnerability, we don't show the best version of ourselves. I think it's not just about people treading water, helping people survive. It's really what do we have available to us that lets us thrive? If we're aware of VUCA, then of course we can be at choice. What kept coming up for me is our values, so the V in my VUCA, in what I call VUCA Tools, is Values. What do I deeply value that's going to give me a compass, something to true back to when I'm uncertain and when things change? How will I make decisions? Whether it's an individual leader or an organization or a team, if we know our values, that's going to help us stay true to those values, and really to have a place of certainty and a foundation, a place to stand.

Meg: Yes, it's grounding.

Ann: That's the exact verb I thought—Values are grounding. Then the U stands for Us. We're not in this alone, you know? There are lots of other people willing to help us, to give us feedback, to share their perspectives. Most of us work on teams, either small teams like partnerships or very big teams. The Us, the other people who can fill in the gaps, help us feel at ease even when we are fearful or uncertain.

Meg: When you said that, even though we're talking about business, I thought about our audience and I thought about how many coaches in this uncertain world work individually or work in their own businesses, yet there are partnerships that we can

213

become involved in, and organizations. Are you tapping into the ICF organization in your area, or are you connecting in online communities of coaching professionals?

Even though we're focusing on the business, that arose for me if you're feeling alone out there in the audience in your business-building as a coach, there is Us in the coaching profession as well.

Ann: Yes, I think you're exactly right. The Us has ended up surprising me a little bit, if that's possible, because sometimes it is another coach. Sometimes it's, as you know from reading the book, a horse. And sometimes it is an organization, somebody that has the answers that I don't have. So that's what the U is.

Then the C is Curiosity, and when you think about the volume of things that leaders are asked to do, that all of us are asked to do, part of what's overwhelming is just the sheer volume and complexity. When we don't know, most of us don't feel at ease. We want to know. We want to be sure.

Curiosity helps us to feel like we're moving forward, to know. I might not know now but I can ask questions, and I can learn. That way I'm going to figure it out. Curiosity is a tool that lets us learn.

Meg: And that leads us to clarity, using that curiosity to get a little more clarity.

Ann: Yes, exactly. And then the A won't surprise you at all. It's Aspirations. My first experience of hearing about VUCA actually was from a government leader who shared it with me, and it was very much about the threat of VUCA. I thought, wow, if it's a threat, then I know that we're going to tend to freeze or flee or try to fight. And when we focus on the problem, we make ourselves small. We may freeze or try to avoid it. What works better is to really think, "Well, where do I want to be?" I might not like this feeling of vulnerability, but what **do** I want? In the case of the team in the book, they want to have a thriving company again, to work as a team.

It's the notion that now I'm not a victim anymore. Now I'm looking ahead and seeing my vision for where I'm headed, my aspirations. And that's not grounding, not grounding at all. That's movement, and we already have the grounding of values. So now we get to move forward to where we want to go.

Meg: You do such a nice job with your book telling it in a story fashion. I think people love stories and we learn from stories. So for those of you who haven't read Ann's first book on team coaching, which is *Being Coached*, I really encourage that you read it. It was one of my favorite group and team coaching books that I've ever read, and you bring in these dynamic characters. And now this book brings back our friends from *Being Coached*.

Can you tell me a little bit from your perspective as an author, what was it like to write this, to revisit your characters, and have grown them? *VUCA Tools* is about three years beyond the first book, so it's kind of visiting our friends again. Maybe I had some reactions to some of the characters, I've got to be honest. What was that like for you?

Ann: It's been really fun. You're right, about three years of their lives have passed. About three years of my life has passed since the first book as well. The leaders actually got to a really good place in the first book, made a lot of progress with coaching one another and being coached as a team or as a group. They got to a really good place, yet now three years later, they're in a different place, right? It's a VUCA world, so things have changed. The terrain's a little different, and though they're approaching it much more effectively than they would have five years ago, they're not feeling as good as they did three years earlier. So it's been cool to see what's changed for them, where they've been in the last three years.

I mentioned this to you before, but as I was writing sometimes I'd wake up in the morning and [realize something]. Jack would have decided he's going to go to an equine coaching session, and I'd have no idea Jack would decide that; it would surprise me. So the characters do have a life of their own and personalities of their own, and they each have strengths. And, especially when they are feeling vulnerable, they have bad habits they go back to, which might be arrogance or being a control freak or a perfectionist, or it might be finger-pointing. We all have that, bad habits—playing small, lots of different bad habits that when we feel stressed we go back to.

Meg: So I'm curious—in many ways I would think that writing these characters is a bit like having children. I mean, you're sort of growing them and developing them. I told you that I reacted to some of them. I'm wondering if you by any chance had favorites or ones that spoke particularly to Ann?

Ann: You know, I think Raj is still one of my favorites. Raj is not a senior leader; he's a mid-level leader in the organization, and he's just grown so much. I love Raj. He's curious. He loves neuroscience, and I love neuroscience. He's just got a nice manner, and he's grown a lot in his confidence, so I love Raj.

I feel compassion for Jack. He's trying to lead a company. Jack loves to be in control, and there's so much outside of his control, and he's having to grapple with that. Jack's not always a sympathetic character, but I love Jack. I love his willingness to struggle with not being in control, being the one who's calling the shots and yet feeling out of control.

Meg: What I also like about Jack is his willingness to be open to the coaching process, and that he opened up his entire team to coaching. He works really hard to allow input and thank people for their input, and be open even if it makes him uncomfortable. So there's a level of vulnerability in him and openness to his team that I find inspirational.

The above is an edited excerpt of an interview with the author by Meg Rentschler for her podcast **STaR Coaches**. To listen to the entire podcast, go to http://www.starcoachshow.com/.

NOTES

1   VUCA is a well-known acronym for Volatility, Uncertainty, Complexity, and Ambiguity—all qualities of the changing reality of our world. Numerous references exist to VUCA, both in the military context where it originated and in a business context. *Harvard Business Review*'s digital series of articles is an excellent starting place to learn more.

- Eric Kail, "Leading Effectively in a VUCA Environment: V Is for Volatility," *Harvard Business Review*, November 3, 2010, http://blogs.hbr.org/frontline-leadership/2010/11/leading-in-a-vuca-environment.html.
- Eric Kail, "Leading Effectively in a VUCA Environment: U Is for Uncertainty," *Harvard Business Review*, November 10, 2010, http://blogs.hbr.org/frontline-leadership/2010/11/leading-in-a-vuca-environment-1.html.
- Eric Kail, "Leading Effectively in a VUCA Environment: C Is for Complexity," *Harvard Business Review*, December 3, 2010, http://blogs.hbr.org/frontline-leadership/2010/12/leading-effectively-in-a-vuca.html.
- Eric Kail, "Leading Effectively in a VUCA Environment: A Is for Ambiguity," *Harvard Business Review*, January 6, 2011, http://blogs.hbr.org/frontline-leadership/2011/01/leading-effectively-in-a-vuca-1.html.

2   It's not necessary to have read our earlier book as a foundation for benefiting from this one. However, if you'd like more context and to learn more about group and team coaching, I encourage you to read Ann V. Deaton and Holly Williams, *Being Coached: Group and Team Coaching from the Inside* (Magus Group, 2014).

3   "Business Fables: The End," by Kevin Evers, was in the July–August 2013 issue of *Harvard Business Review*. Evers's basic point is that stories should show, not tell. I trust I've done that here, and that Evers and others can still enjoy a good story that helps them to see opportunities for choosing, and for implementing effective tools rather than feeling victimized by VUCA.

4   There are many references to VUCA in *Harvard Business Review*. One straightforward and concise article is "What VUCA Really Means for You" by Nathan Bennett and G. James Lemoine. Because it is easily accessible, Ted suggests this as an intro to his colleagues.

5   This list of desired results created by the Tech Environments team is similar to the aspirations of many senior leadership teams for their organizations. By framing the list as outcomes rather than problems and giving each a one-word label, this list of six is made more memorable and motivating.

6   Sustainability has become a buzzword in the business world, in addition to its applications to the environment and economic growth. With a focus on global growth, the UN Brundtland Commission in 1987 defined sustainable development as "development that meets the needs of the present without compromising the ability of future generations to meet their own needs." In the context of VUCA Tools, Edgar's goal for Tech Environments is a strong parallel—to ensure the company is set up to thrive in the future while also addressing more urgent concerns.

7   According to Equus Coaching Master Facilitator Beth Herman, equine coaching offers the opportunity for leaders to:

1.   Notice your internal dialogue that can keep you from reading others' signals

2. Clarify and express your vision so you can create what you really want
3. Practice inspiring others to join you and follow your lead
4. Deal with daily pressures by learning to stay calm and centered in stressful situations
5. Enhance your relationship and communication with everyone. http://ebhermanconsulting.com/equus-coaching/

   Equine coaching is not for everyone, but is an impactful way for an individual leader or a team to have a potentially transformative, and invariably memorable, experience.

8   Amygdala hijacking is a term coined by Daniel Goleman in *Emotional Intelligence: Why It Can Matter More than IQ* (1996). Recognizing that the primitive, survival-oriented parts of our brain are triggered by social threats as well as physical ones, Goleman highlighted the importance of self-awareness in understanding our own triggers and managing our emotions. For more on neuroscience, see Chapter 44 in Part 3, "Resources."

9   David Emerald, *The Power of TED* (*The Empowerment Dynamic)*, 10th Anniversary Edition (Smashwords, 2016).

    Here, Donna is recommending *The Power of TED** as a resource that offers both a methodology and a vocabulary to shift from feeling victimized by people or situations to being empowered to move forward effectively. In our earlier book, *Being Coached: Group and Team Coaching from the Inside*, several of the leaders at Tech Environments used principles of TED* to shift from being critical to focusing on desired outcomes. In addition to the TED* book, in-person and online courses provide structures and actionable strategies to bring the concepts of TED* to life in organizations. More resources can be found at http://powerofted.com and https://elearning.powerofted.com/. If you choose to order the course, use this coupon code to get a $50 discount: adeat$50

10 Judith E. Glaser, *Conversational Intelligence: How Great Leaders Build Trust and Get Extraordinary Results* (Routledge, 2016). The approach of Double-Clicking is highlighted in Chapter 9, "A Toolkit for Level III Conversations."

11 Comprehending the underlying biology of emotions and relationships strengthens the perception of these "soft" areas as tangible and important. In Chapter 2 of *Conversational Intelligence: How Great Leaders Build Trust and Get Extraordinary Results*, Judith E. Glaser provides an easily followed explanation of the underlying neuroscience that Raj is sharing with Kim here of the neurochemical changes we undergo when under stress and when experiencing well-being.

12 Chapter 3 of *Conversational Intelligence* highlights how we move from distrust back to trust.

13 Three Vital Questions is an online course that can be accessed at https://elearning.powerofted.com/. Use this coupon code to get a $50 discount: adeat$50

14 An understandable approach to the neuroscience of relationship and conversation can be found throughout Judith E. Glaser, *Conversational Intelligence: How Great Leaders Build Trust and Get Extraordinary Results* (Routledge, 2016). The book is readable and easy to apply. For those who want to go deeper, explore the courses and other resources at http://www.ciqcoach.com/ and www.conversationalintelligence.com.

15 The nonprofit organization Start with Decency is the brainchild of Ed Stern, MSM. Ed is a leadership coach who was looking for ways that each of us can take action to build more bridges across our differences. Start with Decency is an organization that strives to

create awareness, conversations, and recognition of kind and decent actions that bring us together and help us to leverage the best of both. More information and bumper stickers and other visual cues for inciting kindness can be found at www.startwithdecency.org.

16 Barry Johnson, *Polarity Management: Identifying and Managing Unsolvable Problems* (Human Resource Development Press, 1992). Barry also has a new book due out soon entitled *AND, How to Leverage Polarity, Paradox or Dilemma*

17 Common goals for leaders when they experience equine coaching include becoming a more confident, collaborative, or patient leader, or learning how to read an audience. The horses seem to have an intuitive sense of what is needed, and respond accordingly. The coach supports each leader in seeing and articulating what they learned from the experience, and how they want to put their learning into action outside of the horse ring. Learn more about the power of equine coaching at http://coachingwithhorses.com/.

18 Leaders often learn tools, and then fail to apply them when situations arise. Here, Ted catches himself focusing on a problem, and recognizes that this will distract him from the objective for the meeting by generating judgment and negativity, a downward spiral. In choosing to hold himself accountable for focusing differently, he tests the expectation that doing so will yield a more positive and sustainable outcome. To learn more, read David Emerald, *Power of TED* (*The Empowerment Dynamic)*, 10th Anniversary Edition (Smashwords, 2016).

19 Fulvia Montresor, "The 7 Technologies Changing Your World," World Economic Forum, January 19, 2016, https://www.weforum.org/agenda/2016/01/a-brief-guide-to-the-technologies-changing-world/.

20 Judith E. Glaser, *Conversational Intelligence: How Great Leaders Build Trust and Get Extraordinary Results* (Routledge, 2016).

21 When Lynn and Donna saw the value of The Empowerment Dynamic, they shared it with the rest of the Tech Environments team. Here, Ted is referring to the "3 Vital Questions," an online course to learn the basics of The Empowerment Dynamic, highlighting three critical areas to focus on in relationships. http://powerofted.com/wp-content/uploads/2011/12/3VQ-Flyer-FINAL-050615A.pdf

22 Barry Johnson's creation of polarity principles and the polarity mapping process enables teams to leverage their differences. To learn more about polarity thinking and the PACT assessment, go to http://www.polaritypartnerships.com/

23 When I first developed the idea of VUCA Tools™ as an approach to responding to VUCA, I had no idea that others might think to do the same. At least two other leadership experts have landed on a similar notion that VUCA needs an antidote, and that its solution might well leverage the same four letters as the original acronym. Both Bob Johansen and Bill George highlight the importance of leaders having Vision and developing Understanding, the first two letters. I see Vision and Understanding as analogous to my own VUCA Tools of Aspirations and Curiosity. For the reader's ease, I've listed all three VUCA solution approaches in the table below. Johansen's book, and his collaboration with the Center for Creative Leadership, includes a rich how-to for leaders intent on immersing themselves in becoming more effective. George's short article on VUCA 2.0 highlights the importance of leaders being courageous, a critical attribute for facing the challenges of VUCA.

Ann V. Deaton	*VUCA Tools for a VUCA World: Developing Leaders and Teams for Sustainable Results,* 2018	Values Us Curiosity Aspirations	VUCA Tools
Bob Johansen	*Leaders Make the Future* (2012, 2nd edition)	Vision Understanding Clarity Agility	VUCA Prime
Bill George	VUCA 2.0: A Strategy for Steady Leadership in an Unsteady World, Forbes.com, Feb. 17, 2017	Vision Understanding Courage Adaptability	VUCA 2.0

65842619R00133

Made in the USA
Middletown, DE
04 September 2019